Penguin Critical Studies

C000143991

Troilus and Cressida

Peter Hyland is Associate Professor of English at Huron College in the University of Western Ontario, Canada. Educated at the University of Wales and McMaster University, he has taught in universities in Iran, Japan and Singapore, and has been Senior Fellow at the Centre for Reformation and Renaissance Studies, Toronto. His publications include *Disguise and Role-playing in Ben Jonson's Drama* (1977) and (as editor) *Discharging the Canon: Cross-cultural Readings in Literature* (1986), as well as many articles on Renaissance drama.

Penguin Critical Studies
Joint Advisory Editors:
Stephen Coote and Bryan Loughrey

William Shakespeare

Troilus and Cressida

Peter Hyland

Penguin Books

PENGUIN BOOKS

Published by the Penguin Group
27 Wrights Lane, London W8 5TZ, England
Viking Penguin Inc., 40 West 23rd Street, New York, New York 10010, USA
Penguin Books Australia Ltd, Ringwood, Victoria, Australia
Penguin Books Canada Ltd, 2801 John Street, Markham, Ontario, Canada L3R 1B4
Penguin Books (NZ) Ltd, 182–190 Wairau Road, Auckland 10, New Zealand

Penguin Books Ltd, Registered Offices: Harmondsworth, Middlesex, England

First published 1989
10 9 8 7 6 5 4 3 2 1

Made and printed in Great Britain by
Richard Clay Ltd, Bungay, Suffolk
Filmset in Monophoto Times

For Theresa
and for Brendan and Robert

Contents

1. Introduction

Troilus and Cressida is Shakespeare's most puzzling work and, if we look at its theatrical and critical history, it appears that it has the dubious distinction of being amongst his least-liked plays. As to its stage history, it is by no means certain that the play was acted even in Shakespeare's own time; the evidence is, as we shall see, somewhat ambiguous, but there is no record of any contemporary performance. John Dryden produced a version of the play for the later seventeenth century, *Troilus and Cressida, or Truth Found Too Late* (1679), but he in effect re-wrote it, for in order to reveal its 'excellent thoughts', he had to remove a 'heap of rubbish' under which they 'lay wholly bury'd'. As far as is known, there was no other production in England until 1907, when a performance at the Great Queen Street Theatre in London convinced the reviewer for *The Times* that the play was 'better left unacted'. Fortunately, directors and companies have not been deterred by this view, and in the twentieth century the play has been seen in a number of productions, though it is still far from being amongst the most popular works in the Shakespearean canon.

Troilus and Cressida has not fared much better at the hands of critics. Dryden, who thought that the play was a tragedy, was worried because 'The chief persons, who give name to the Tragedy, are left alive: Cressida is false, and is not punish'd.' This would appear to mean that if the play is a tragedy it is a failure. But Dryden may have been mistaken about its nature, for critics since his time have not all been convinced that the play is a tragedy. The problem is not made easier by the evidence of the earliest editions. The original Quarto title-page (1609) calls it a history, as does an entry for the same year in the Stationers' Register. However, the epistle that prefaces some copies of the Quarto (also 1609) describes the play as a comedy. The editors of the first collected edition of Shakespeare's plays, the Folio of 1623, placed it between the histories and the tragedies, although their original intention, apparently, was to place it amongst the tragedies. What this ought to suggest to us, perhaps, is that the Elizabethans had a rather more flexible attitude toward genre than much modern criticism is willing to allow them. Nonetheless, much of the commentary on the play has attempted to read it in terms of genre, as a tragedy or as a comedy, and either has failed to give a satisfactory account of it, or has found the play itself to be a (more or less noble)

1

failure. Some critics have tried to deal with the complexities that make the play break out of the strict boundaries of traditional genre by seeing it as satire; this approach has sometimes yielded more satisfying results, but it raises problems of its own.

Part of the difficulty here arises, perhaps, from a critical inclination to evaluate an artistic work in terms of its unity, to impose upon it a preconception of desirable form that gives a full account, or 'reading', of it that will, in some way, 'complete' it. One may feel, however, that an endeavour of this nature tends to limit a literary work, that what most excites or moves us about the literature we enjoy is precisely its resistance to such reduction, the way in which it bursts through the boundaries that we try to impose upon it. If this is so, then *Troilus and Cressida* is all the more intriguing, for it allows us no point of completion, but insistently challenges us to question any statement we make about it, just as it challenges the statements that its characters make. It provides a framework, a site of conflict, for a whole complex of ideas that are continually weighed and scrutinized from a range of opposing points of view, none of which, finally, is given privileged status over all others.

A further source of preconceptions that may impede an understanding of the play is the very idea of 'Shakespeare', the great poet of England who, according to his contemporary Ben Jonson, 'was not of an age, but for all time' (we do not know what Shakespeare himself thought of this idea). This Shakespeare is less a man than a symbol, the great genius of absolute artistic integrity who knows everything, shedding his light on the world from a vast distance, as Matthew Arnold sees him in his sonnet 'Shakespeare':

> Others abide our question. Thou art free.
> We ask and ask – Thou smilest and art still,
> Out-topping knowledge.

All the works of this man are somehow 'right'; he is the moral and patriotic spokesman for his country, creator of a monolithic and consistent body of writing, who holds up all that is good for his audience's admiration and approval: romantic love, ideas of constancy, heroism, the power of reason. Much traditional commentary on Shakespeare has taken this image for granted, to the great disadvantage of *Troilus and Cressida*, which appears to mock so many of the things that Shakespeare was presumed to hold dear. The play has been explained away as an aberration, written when the dramatist was undergoing some personal (though unknown and unproven) suffering, and there have even been attempts (as with other 'unlikeable' plays, such as *Titus Andronicus*) to

2

argue that parts of it were written by other, lesser dramatists, Thomas Dekker and Henry Chettle (who did indeed write a play on the subject), or George Chapman and John Marston.

Recent criticism has forced reading of Shakespeare back to some fundamental questions, the primary one being: Whose Shakespeare are we dealing with? – the dramatist who has been taken over by established authority as representing its values, or a different Shakespeare, inextricably related to the social, material and ideological context of his own time? Furthermore, when we look at the play itself we have to ask a similar question: Which *Troilus and Cressida*? For a dramatic text is not a static, fixed object; it is the outline for a performance that will include action, spectacle and music, and that allows a great deal of freedom of interpretation to director and actors. And even as a written text, *Troilus and Cressida* exists in different versions. For example, both Quarto and Folio versions end with a kind of epilogue, spoken by Pandarus, complaining about the way the world (in the form of Troilus) has treated his good intentions. This epilogue is initiated by a couplet spoken by Troilus, in which he angrily dismisses the old pandar:

> Hence, broker-lackey! Ignomy and shame
> Pursue thy life, and live aye with thy name!
> (V.10.33–4)

In the Folio version, however, these same lines appear also at the end of V.3 – that is, Pandarus is dismissed at this point in the play. Now clearly this provides two possible acting versions: a director must either cut the lines at the end of V.3, or cut out the epilogue. In the former case, the final words of the play are left to its chief comic figure, and the impression the audience takes away will be affected by this. In the latter case, the final words will be the speech in which Troilus expresses his determination to take the place of Hector in order to avenge the death of the murdered hero and crush the enemies of Troy – an ending with a very different tone. So which of these is the 'real' *Troilus and Cressida*? There is, of course, no answer; we have to make a choice about how we see Shakespeare and how we see his play, but we must be constantly aware that other choices are possible – which may very well be one of the things that the play itself sets out to demonstrate.

One thing that should become clear when we dismiss the idea of Shakespeare and his plays as a monolithic ideal entity is that, whatever else he might have been, he was a practical craftsman, working – like all the other professional dramatists of his time – with the blood and dirt of real life. He was constrained by a great many things: the economic necessities and insecurities of earning a living, the limitations of the physical structure of the theatre, the nature and particular demands of the actors for whom he was writing, the interests of the audience, the need to keep up with new fashions and to compete with rival acting companies, and, no doubt, the perennial struggle against deadlines and writer's block. He wrote his plays for an audience that had quite different expectations from those that a modern audience might hold. His audience wasn't made up of tourists and examination classes sitting in awed (or bored) silence, watching a distant, framed performance of a set text. The theatres were rowdy, carnivalesque places, where (if we are to believe on the one hand such admittedly hostile contemporary witnesses as the Puritans Stephen Gosson and Philip Stubbes, and on the other playwrights themselves such as Thomas Dekker) whores and pickpockets plied their trades, and eating, drinking and smoking went on throughout the performance. In some cases, fashionable wits were able to purchase seats on the stage itself in order to rival the play in making public spectacles of themselves. They were people who would have had no hesitation about making felt their disapproval of a bad performance or a bad play.

We cannot now know what was the occasion for the writing of *Troilus and Cressida*. The absence of any evidence that the play was actually performed may suggest that it was not a success, and certainly on first acquaintance it may not seem to be very appealing. It is difficult to admire the nominal hero and heroine, the one self-deluded, the other shallow and pliable. The larger-than-life opponents in the best-known war in history, subject of the great classical epics, are here presented as devious, hollow, or stupid. The play is full of speeches delivered in elevated style and presenting lofty ideals, which yet seem to be negated by the selfish motives, the dishonesties and betrayals, of the majority of the characters. But it is these very ambiguities that make the play so intriguing. It cannot be reduced to a simple formula that will allow for a satisfying reading. It examines opposing attitudes, allowing them to interrogate one another. It allows idealism to be represented, and to be questioned by cynicism and undercut by reality, but it refuses to settle on any middle ground. It relentlessly exposes the gap between what men say and how they act: it shows that a man may eloquently present the case for order and harmony and yet act himself with a deviousness that promotes the opposite of harmony, and that rational argument does not necessarily lead to rational action. It is a complex intellectual play, but it is also a play about doomed human beings, doomed by time and their own unstable natures – doomed, indeed, by the very fact that they are human. Whether life is seen as contemptible or noble, a comic or a tragic business, depends entirely on one's point of view, but any point of view ought to recognize the possibility of others. If, therefore, after seeing or reading *Troilus and Cressida*, we are left with a feeling of uneasiness at its refusal (not its failure) to allow us an unequivocal response, perhaps it is that very uneasiness that gives the play its significance.

2. Context and Materials

Troilus and Cressida in its Context

There is general scholarly agreement that *Troilus and Cressida* was written between 1601 and 1603. By this time Shakespeare had produced his two historical tetralogies and the series of romantic comedies that ends with *Twelfth Night*. He had also completed *Hamlet*, his first major experiment in tragedy. *Troilus and Cressida* is the first of three plays (the others are *All's Well That Ends Well* and *Measure for Measure*) that intervene between *Hamlet* and the other major tragedies, and that have perennially puzzled critics. These three plays have a form that is akin to comedy, but they deal with issues often considered alien to comedy, they are dark and ambiguous in atmosphere, and each has an ending that disturbs rather than satisfies. They have consequently been treated as a group, and labelled 'dark comedies', 'bitter comedies', or 'problem plays'. All these terms, although they do suggest something about the nature of the plays, may, however, be thought to indicate problems with critical strategy as much as with the plays themselves.

By 1601 Shakespeare had made himself a remarkably successful playwright on the London scene. Born in Stratford-on-Avon in 1564 and educated there, probably in a grammar school, he had moved to London sometime before 1592, apparently finding employment as an actor before he became a playwright. Little is known about these early years of his life, or about his early stage career; the first reference to him as a professional dramatist comes in an attack by Robert Greene, himself a playwright, who clearly saw Shakespeare as a rival and resented his success:

> There is an upstart crow, beautified with our feathers, that with his *tiger's heart wrapped in a player's hide* supposes he is as well able to bombast out a blank verse as the best of you, and being an absolute Johannes-factotum is in his own conceit the only Shake-scene in a country.

What this demonstrates, apart from Greene's spleen, is that by 1592 Shakespeare had established himself well enough in the London theatre for Greene to see him as a serious rival. He had certainly written his earliest history plays (the 'tiger's heart' reference is to *3 Henry VI*), and probably *The Taming of the Shrew* and *The Comedy of Errors*, and the blood-soaked tragedy *Titus Andronicus*, demonstrating his versatility with popular forms even at this early stage.

6

Soon after Greene's attack on him, in 1593 Shakespeare found a patron in Henry Wriothesley, Earl of Southampton. As we shall see, the relationship between the theatre, its writers, and powerful figures at court was a crucial one. Southampton was a brilliant, handsome young man who encouraged many writers and scholars; Shakespeare dedicated his narrative poem *Venus and Adonis* to him and, in the following year, *The Rape of Lucrece*. Shakespeare's non-dramatic writing was merely a sideline, however, and he continued his theatrical career as both actor and dramatist, joining the company of players known as the Lord Chamberlain's Men in 1594. The protection of a court figure was as essential for the acting companies as patronage was for a writer, and the companies bore such names as Lord Strange's Men, the Admiral's Men and the Queen's Men. There had been no permanent theatre in London until 1576; before that the acting companies had been itinerant players, performing wherever they could find a platform and an audience. They were still, in Shakespeare's time, widely considered as vagabonds, just as the theatre was thought by many to be an immoral and dangerous place. The actors held a very ambiguous situation, therefore, as objects of suspicion, and were made legitimate mainly by their noble protectors.

The Lord Chamberlain's Men was the most successful acting company of the time, largely, no doubt, because of Shakespeare's contribution; so respected were they that when King James I came to the throne they were honoured by being allowed to change their name to the King's Men. In 1599 they moved to the famous Globe Theatre, which they had built for themselves, and Shakespeare himself became owner of a tenth share in the theatre and the company. This demonstrates how important Shakespeare was to the company, but it also shows how important the commercial (as opposed to artistic) success of the company must have been to Shakespeare. It was the source of his later great prosperity, and he remained with the company until he retired in 1612 to the fine house he had bought in Stratford called New Place, where he died in 1616.

In his own time Shakespeare appears to have been the most popular of the many dramatists active in both the public and private companies, and clearly knew what his audience wanted. Today we think of him as the greatest of artists, but it is not likely that he looked on himself in this way. The theatre was a means of earning a living, and many of its crucial developments appear to have been economic rather than artistic. For example, one of the key events in the theatre history of the time was the opening of Burbage's Theatre in 1576 because this, the first permanent public theatre, fixed the relationships between stage, building and audience, relationships which had previously been quite casual. This fixing of the playing space must have had an influence on the writers, who now knew what they were writing for, and it must have had an influence on the relationship between actors and audience, not only in terms of the space between them, but also because it allowed for the formation of a regular local audience. But the main motive for building Burbage's Theatre was to make sure that all those who saw the play paid – something that had not been possible when the travelling companies had had to make do with whatever stage they could find.

Although Shakespeare's writing is associated mainly with the public theatres, we must note that there were private theatres too. These had their origin in the boys' grammar schools, the universities and the Inns of Court, but most particularly in the boys' choirs recruited for such institutions as the Chapel Royal and St Paul's Cathedral. By Shakespeare's time these companies had become as commercial as the public companies, so the word 'private' is a little misleading; the private theatres were only private in the sense that they were more expensive, but they consequently catered for a wealthier and therefore more erudite, specialized and sophisticated audience. There were differences in playhouse structure, because most of the private theatres were essentially banqueting halls and were completely enclosed, unlike the open-air public theatres; this allowed for more elaborate special effects, and encouraged different kinds of plays from those performed in the public playhouses. But it is easy to overestimate the differences; there was a good deal of overlap, and many plays written for public theatres were also performed in private theatres. As we shall see, this fact may have a bearing upon Shakespeare's original intention in writing *Troilus and Cressida*.

The nature of the audience must have been as important an influence as the structure of the theatre edifice on the kinds of play a dramatist would produce. There is some disagreement about who it was that made up the audience attending the public theatres. It used to be thought that Shakespeare's audience represented a cross-section of Elizabethan society, from the aristocracy, through the middle classes, to the lower classes of workmen, the latter paying a penny to stand in the auditorium and hence called 'groundlings'. It has recently been argued, however, that this charge of a penny, small as it may seem to us today, would have excluded many of the lower classes; furthermore, the fact that the public theatres depended on natural light meant that performances had to take place in the afternoon, which suggests that only those who had a certain amount of leisure could attend – that the audience, in fact, was a comparatively privileged one.

The complex and often difficult experience of reading a Shakespearean play indicates to us that his audience wanted more than simply to be entertained. Though less sophisticated, perhaps, than the audience attending the private companies it was still a metropolitan audience, with many of its members familiar with the court, and one that would have been well informed on political issues and acutely aware of what went on in powerful circles. The dramatists were often able to comment on topical issues (and sometimes stepped over the fine boundary into propaganda), feeling protected by the fiction of the play, though it is clear that they were performing a delicate balancing act; Ben Jonson, for example, was imprisoned for his contribution to a play of 1597 called *The Isle of Dogs* which was considered by the Privy Council to contain 'very seditious and slanderous matter'. Again, we can see the curious contradiction in the relationship of the theatres to established authority; just as the actors were vagrants who had aristocratic protection, the theatres were tolerated because they had royal support, but they were also the object of suspicion amongst the increasingly powerful protestant element of the middle classes. Indeed, except for the Blackfriars Theatre, the authorities of the City of London allowed no playhouse to be built within the City boundaries during the sixteenth century.

One can see many reasons, of course, why the guardians of order should worry about the potential disorder that could be created by the playhouses. They brought together large numbers of people, and although scripts were censored through the Revels Office, it was impossible fully to control what was said or acted out on the stage. One extreme view of the dangers of plays comes from the Puritan pamphleteer Philip Stubbes in *The Anatomie of Abuses* (1583):

And these be the fruits of plays and interludes, for the most part. And whereas, you say, there are good examples to be learnt in them: truly, so there are; if you will learn falsehood; if you will learn cozenage; if you will learn to deceive; if you will learn to play the hypocrite, to cog, to lie and falsify; if you will learn to jest, laugh and fleer, to grin, to nod and mow; if you will learn to play the Vice, to swear, tear and blaspheme both heaven and earth; if you will learn to become a bawd, unclean, and to devirginate maids, to deflower honest wives; if you will learn to murder, flay, kill, pick, steal, rob and rove; if you will learn to rebel against princes, to commit treasons, to consume treasures, to practise idleness, to sing and talk of bawdy love and venery; if you will learn to deride, scoff, mock and flout, to flatter and smooth; if you will learn to play the whoremaster, the glutton, drunkard, or incestuous person; if you will learn to become proud, haughty and arrogant; and finally, if you will learn to contemn God and all His laws, to care neither for Heaven nor Hell, and to commit all kinds of sin and mischief, you need to go to no other school, for all these good examples may you see painted before your eyes in interludes and plays.

We may feel that Stubbes's tone is somewhat hysterical, that he exaggerates the affective power of the theatre. Yet we must remember that Elizabethan society was not especially stable, that there were thousands of vagrants or masterless men in London who were seen to pose a perennial threat to established moral and political order, and that the theatres offered a parallel reality to the official one, presenting images of inversion and transformation that might very well stir up a volatile audience.

Indeed, at the time during which Shakespeare was writing *Troilus and Cressida*, England's stability must have seemed especially threatened. Queen Elizabeth clearly had few more years to live (and died, in fact, in 1603); she had no heirs, never having married, and there was no clear idea who would succeed her. In 1601 her one-time favourite, Robert Devereux, Earl of Essex, led an unsuccessful rebellion against her and was executed for it. In the same year there was something close to revolt in the House of Commons over the question of monopolies, and only the Queen's political genius deflected this challenge to the authority of the Crown. It is, perhaps, this larger insecurity in the state, rather than any hypothetical personal suffering, that is reflected in the darker tone of *Troilus and Cressida*.

What is generally taken to be the first reference to Shakespeare's *Troilus and Cressida* (although no author is named) appears in an entry in the Stationers' Register for 7 February 1603 on behalf of a Mr Roberts, who wished to print 'the book of Troilus and Cresseda as it is acted by my Lord Chamberlain's Men'. He apparently did not receive permission, however, because the play was not published; nor is there any record of performances by the Lord Chamberlain's Men. We next hear of the play in 1609, again in the Stationers' Register, when Richard Bonion and Henry Walleys requested permission to publish 'The history of Troylus & Cressida', which they did in that year. The Quarto text of 1609 bears an original title-page which also describes the play as a history, and claims that it was 'acted by the Kings Majesties servants at the Globe'. This presumably refers to the performances of the Lord Chamberlain's Men (who had subsequently received royal patronage and had become the King's Men) mentioned in the 1603 entry in the Stationers' Register. However, this title-page was cancelled, perhaps because the publishers were informed that there had been no performances at the Globe, and it was replaced by the title-page that expands the play's title to *The Famous*

Historie of Troylus and Cresseid, and directs the reader's attention to 'the conceited wooing of Pandarus Prince of Licia' – that is, to the comic aspect of the play. Inserted into this edition is an epistle that insists that the play is a comedy, but also claims that it is 'a new play, never staled with the stage, never clapper-clawed with the palms of the vulgar'. The question of the play's genre is further complicated by the version of it that appears in the first collection of Shakespeare's works, the 1623 Folio, which has as its title *The Tragedie of Troylus and Cressida.* The play is inserted between the histories and the tragedies, but it is clear that the editors' first intention had been to place it amongst the tragedies.

The confusion about the play's genre is something we shall have to look at elsewhere; the problems about its dating and whether or not it was ever acted concern us here. The 1603 entry in the Stationers' Register means that a manuscript version of *Troilus and Cressida* must have existed at that time; it cannot now be known how precisely this version was represented by the 1609 Quarto edition. Unless it was a piece of dishonest advertising, the epistle claiming that this was a new play must also have been written in 1603, but it is difficult to imagine why it was written, or by whom. It does seem to demonstrate that the claims that the play had been performed at the Globe were mistaken, as does the cancellation of the original title-page. The epistle's rather self-conscious wit and its contempt for 'the vulgar' (presumably the audience at the public theatre), along with the great amount of strenuous argument in the play itself (this is the most intellectually taxing play in the Shakespearean canon), have suggested to some scholars that *Troilus and Cressida* was written for private performance, probably at one of the Inns of Court. The play's apparent cynicism would no doubt have had more appeal to an audience of worldly-wise young lawyers than to the larger public audience. But none of this is anything more than conjecture. The fact is that there is no record either of private or public performance, and it seems likely that the play was not a success.

Materials

One question that now arises is: Of what possible interest could the rather remote story of the Trojan War be to Shakespeare or to the Elizabethan audience? In fact, from medieval times England had had a very intimate concern with the matter of Troy, and in the last few years of the sixteenth century there had been something of a revival of interest. In 1598 George Chapman had begun to publish his translation of Homer's *Iliad* (a project he approached with a solemnity Shakespeare may well have thought deserved to be mocked). Plays about Troy had been popular in the 1590s, and Shakespeare's immediate stimulus to write may have been the success of a play about Troilus and Cressida (now no longer extant) written in 1599 by Thomas Dekker and Henry Chettle for the Admiral's Men, a rival company.

English interest in Troy went back at least to the twelfth century. In 1136 Geoffrey of Monmouth completed a book entitled *Historia regum Britanniae* (*The History of the Kings of Britain*). According to this book Brutus, the grandson of the Trojan hero Aeneas, came to the island of Albion with a band of Trojan followers, defeated the giants who inhabited it, and re-named it 'Britain' after his own name. He settled on the River Thames and founded the city that is now London, but which he called Troia Nova, or New Troy. From him there descended a race of kings, including the greatest figure of British legend, King Arthur. Geoffrey's strange mixture of myth, legend and history, connecting the mythology of Troy with the mythology of Britain, was tremendously influential; it seems to have been adopted as if it were actual history by later medieval historians, and London was often referred to as 'Trenovant'. Thus for the Middle Ages Troy acted as a potent example to New Troy. That great civilized city, with its topless towers bussing the clouds, presented an image which London liked to feel was reflected in itself. But Troy also stood as a warning, because it had allowed its stability to be corrupted by laxity and decadence until the Greeks were able to destroy it; that is, the causes of its downfall were internal.

English monarchs, including the Tudors, encouraged attempts by historiographers to connect their lineage to Arthur as a means of strengthening their right to rule, and this meant that the royal line stretched back through Arthur to Troy. By the end of the sixteenth century, of course, Geoffrey's tales had been discredited as history, but the connection he had made between the present and the distant past had not been forgotten. The story of Troy still held rich mythic echoes for England, and must have seemed to Shakespeare to stand as a powerful metaphor for a country declining from the Golden Age of Elizabeth's great reign into disorder and uncertainty, and a grimly unpredictable future. This, perhaps, is why he chose to use that part of the Trojan history that tells of the pivotal event necessary for the fall of Troy – the death of Hector – but does not follow it through to the disastrous end itself, since that end is well known and fully indicated by what is dramatized.

The matter of Troy, then, at least in its broad outlines, must have been very familiar to Shakespeare's audience. The story of the heroic battles between Greek and Trojan warriors dates back to Homer, and parts of it could be found also in Virgil's *Aeneid* and Ovid's *Metamorphoses*, both of which Shakespeare would have known. The Homeric story was later modified by accounts of two men who had supposedly participated in the Trojan War, Dictys the Cretan and Dares the Phrygian, though both accounts are apparently fraudulent. The pro-Greek Dictys version appeared in the fourth century A.D.; the Dares version, this one pro-Trojan, appeared two centuries later, and various translations and amplifications of these stories were made in the Middle Ages. The story of Troilus and Cressida is a medieval addition, having no part in the old epic versions of the Troy history. It seems to have made its first (brief) appearance in the twelfth century in Benoît de Sainte-Maure's *Roman de Troie*, but not until Boccaccio's *Il Filostrato* was the full story told. Boccaccio's romance was the main source of Geoffrey Chaucer's *Troilus and Criseyde*.

There is some disagreement about the sources Shakespeare used for his play about the Trojan War. He would almost certainly have known Chapman's translations, and it is well established that he used two medieval English accounts: William Caxton's *Recuyell of the Historyes of Troye*, and John Lydgate's *Troye Booke*. Because of the radical difference between the two poets' attitudes to their material, some scholars have questioned whether Shakespeare used Chaucer's poem, but since this was the best-known account of the lovers, it seems foolish to doubt it. Certainly Chaucer is far more generous to his characters, but Elizabethan readers would have thought of Chaucer's story in the light of its harsher sequel, Robert Henryson's *Testament of Cressid*, which was included in all contemporary editions of Chaucer and was widely believed to have been Chaucer's own work. Henryson's poem is rather more moralistic, taking up the experiences of Cressida after her betrayal of Troilus. Abandoned by Diomedes, she becomes a whore to a number of Greek warriors, and finally, reduced to beggary, she dies of leprosy. By the time that Shakespeare wrote a profoundly negative image of Cressida had been established, and it would have been very difficult for him to treat her with anything like the sympathy Chaucer was able to give her.

While it is not necessary here to identify specific points of connection between Shakespeare's play and its presumed sources, it is necessary to recognize the play's intertextuality. That is, it would have been understood in its relation to the larger literary and mythical history of its materials, and part of its effect would have been dependent on that history. Just as Shakespeare's Cressida would have been understood not only in relation to Chaucer's, but also in relation to the subsequent darkening of the meaning of the figure, so also the burlesquing of the classical heroes could only have had a meaning in relation to a tradition that revered them – although because of the English pro-Trojan bias, derived from the Brutus story, there was indeed a certain hostility in the Renaissance to the Greeks, who were seen as corrupt and treacherous; the term 'merry Greek', used twice by Cressida, was a contemptuous term for a wanton person. This may account for the view once held by many critics that Shakespeare mocks the Greeks but not the Trojans, a view that is, of course, wrong.

Although Shakespeare could change details within the story (for example, he delays the death of Patroclus in order to provide a motivation for Achilles to return to the battle), the larger outline of the story was something that was fixed, and part of the play's effect depends on this too – because the outcome of the events is foreknown by the audience, there is a strong sense of inevitability and fatality. This foreknowledge also imparts comic irony to the lovers' protestations of eternal fidelity at the end of III.2. But Shakespeare was not obliged to include everything – how could he, indeed, when he had to compress events from lengthy and leisurely narrative sources into the brief compass of a stage play? So, while Chaucer was able to allow time for a proper relationship to develop between Troilus and Cressida, and for an examination of Cressida's doubt and anguish over her betrayal of Troilus, the short space of time available to the dramatist to represent these events on the stage makes the relationship as Shakespeare presents it seem all the more shallow, and Cressida's speedy betrayal all the more cynical.

One major change that Shakespeare had to make to the Homeric version of the story is an omission that to some degree affects the motivation of the play. In the *Iliad*, the events take place simultaneously on two levels, the human level of the war between the Greek and Trojan warriors, and the supernatural level of conflict and manipulation between gods and goddesses, each of whom has favourites, and all of whom make frequent intrusions into the human level of action. This means that the causes of many of the things that happen on the human level are unknown to the human agents – they happen because a deity has predicted or promised that they will happen, or has, on a whim or to protect a favourite, interfered with human events. By removing the gods, Shakespeare is able to complicate character by providing a psychological motivation for action – or by withholding motivation, as he does in the case of Achilles' withdrawal from the battle, thus increasing the sense of irrationality.

Shakespeare was not, then, trying merely to dramatize the classical or the medieval versions of the story. His heroes are foolish, self-deceiving and small-minded in comparison with the rather simpler giants of the Homeric epic. The affair between his Troilus and Cressida is very different from that between Chaucer's lovers, not because he failed to understand the specifically medieval preoccupations of Chaucer's poem, as it attempts to explore within terms of Christian orthodoxy an essentially illicit courtly love relationship, but because he saw that medieval courtesy or chivalry had no place in his own time. This is what makes Hector's challenge to the Greeks so ridiculous:

> Hector, in view of Trojans and of Greeks,
> Shall make it good, or do his best to do it,
> He hath a lady, wiser, fairer, truer,
> Than ever Greek did compass in his arms;
> And will tomorrow with his trumpet call,
> Midway between your tents and walls of Troy,
> To rouse a Grecian that is true in love.
>
> (I.3.273–9)

This courtly challenge to single combat seems curiously naive in the context of the brutal war, and it is indeed his attachment to an obsolete code of conduct that brings about Hector's death. Shakespeare apparently had far more ambivalent feelings about his materials than did his predecessors, and he substantially darkened both the martial and the romantic lines of his play as he strove to recreate the ancient story for his own time.

3. The Play

Genre

So much critical energy has been expended in attempts to identify the genre of *Troilus and Cressida* that it would be difficult to avoid the question here, even though answers have rarely been satisfactory. As we have seen, the issue has been complicated from the very beginning by the fact that the play was defined in so many ways by Shakespeare and his original publishers and editors. The Quarto title-pages call the play a history, while the epistle attached to the Quarto indicates that the play is a comedy; the Folio, however, calls it a tragedy. In addition to these possibilities, some critics have added a further one, considering the play to be a satire (or a 'comical satire', or a 'tragical satire'). The problem with attempts to classify the play in terms of preconceived generic terminology (for example by calling it a tragedy and then discussing it as such) is that it will inevitably seem to be a failure, since it does not fit satisfactorily into traditional categories.

Many critics have taken seriously the elevated strain of much of the play, and have followed the Folio editors in thinking of it as a tragedy. The Folio classification, since it was made after his death, may have nothing to say about what Shakespeare thought, although the Folio version of the play does contain the extra final exit for Pandarus in V.3, which implies a revised acting version from which the epilogue was cut. If Pandarus is dismissed at the end of V.3, the play closes with Troilus' speech about Hector's death, which can certainly be seen as pushing towards the tragic. The editors hedged their bets, however, by including both exits for Pandarus, and they may have had doubts about their classification, since they finally placed the play between the histories and the tragedies. Nevertheless, it can be argued that the events of the play are serious and appropriate for tragedy. The larger issue of the fate of Troy was from the earliest telling of the story considered to be tragic matter; the story of Troilus is more ambiguous, but his fate is parallel to that of the city (the name 'Troilus' meaning 'little Troy'), and from medieval readings onwards was understood to echo its tragedy. Although Chaucer's version has frequently been read as ironic comedy, at its conclusion he calls it 'litel myn tragedye'. But if we define the play as tragedy, the question then arises: Who is the tragic hero? The only candidates for this title are Troilus and Hector, the former being the obvious one, since he is the play's nominal hero. But it is difficult to make Troilus into a tragic figure; for one thing, as Dryden pointed out, he doesn't die. More importantly, painful though his experience is, it is not tragic. Every attempt he makes to elevate his situation and feelings is undermined by his comic involvement with Pandarus, and he gains no insight into himself or about the world as a result of his suffering. Hector's death would seem to make him a more legitimate tragic hero, but it is futile and unnecessary (we get no sense of an inexorable movement towards death) and the manner in which it occurs deprives it of any dignity. However repellent the murder of Hector, the feeling it leaves us with is not, finally, tragic.

The Quarto epistle is quite insistent about what kind of play *Troilus and Cressida* is, using the words 'comedy' or 'comical' nine times. Again, however, there is no evidence that Shakespeare had any hand in the composition of the epistle, and since it was apparently used to advertise an unpopular play, it cannot be trusted; indeed, when the epistle's author says that 'the most displeased with plays are pleased with his comedies', he may well be trying to persuade a sceptical audience that this is a comedy and therefore worthy of attention. Any critical attempt to read the play as a comedy comes up against the fact that it is certainly not formally a comedy, at least in the way that such romantic comedies as *As You Like It* and *Twelfth Night* are, with their generally happy endings. Even the two 'bitter comedies' to which *Troilus and Cressida* is frequently linked end in the harmony of marriage or reconciliation. There is no harmony at the end of this play, and although there is certainly comic matter in it, there is also a great deal of matter that is too disturbing to be accommodated in what we would normally think of as comedy.

'True and not true', says Cressida of Pandarus' attempt to describe Troilus' complexion. 'This is, and is not Cressid!' says Troilus after witnessing her infidelity. We might wish to echo this: 'Tragedy and not tragedy'; 'This is, and is not comedy.' The play clearly contains strong elements of both, yet can be defined as neither. It produces its effects, indeed, from what we might call a principle of simultaneity; that is, it acknowledges opposing possibilities and gains its meaning from the tension between them without allowing that tension to be resolved. The audience's response moves it in incompatible directions, and irony is generated in the space between. Consequently, to consider the play as satire seems to hold out more potential for giving an adequate account of it, since satire can coexist with either tragedy or comedy. The play does have much in common with the plays that Ben Jonson was writing at the time, and that he called 'comical satires'. In these plays a satirist-figure who represents in some way the dramatist's own point of view exposes the follies and affectations of the world as it is embodied in the play's characters. Now clearly there is a large satirical element in *Troilus and Cressida*, and the 'Prologue armed' who introduces the play is a direct reference to Jonson's play *The Poetaster* that appeared in 1601 (Jonson's comical satires were in part his weaponry in the so-called 'war of the theatres' that developed between rival companies at the turn of the century; *Troilus and Cressida* has sometimes been seen as Shakespeare's contribution to the quarrel, but the evidence for this is rather thin). The problem with seeing the play as comical satire is that the satirist-figure in the play is Thersites, and while all critics agree that there is much truth in Thersites' satirical broadsides, none is willing to identify him with Shakespeare's point of view.

Satire is most commonly thought of in its relation to comedy, but what distinguishes the satire of *Troilus and Cressida* from the comical satire of Jonson's plays is its philosophical concern with matters that are potentially tragic: its vision of a fallen world presented through the perspective of a perceived ideal, as articulated by Ulysses in his speech on degree, and its sense of the vulnerability of all ideals and all things that men do under the omnipresent threat of time. But any association with the tragic of the satire of this play is insistently undercut by the amount of invective in it, associated mainly with Thersites. This division of satire between the generally disillusioned and saddened vision of the play on the one hand and the envy-driven malice of Thersites on the other corresponds to a widespread misunderstanding amongst Elizabethan writers of the etymology of the word 'satire'. The word was derived from the Latin word *satura*, meaning a dish made up of various ingredients, and as a literary term implied a work containing a variety of topics. Elizabethan writers understood the word as 'satyre', however, and believed it to be derived from the Greek satyr-play, as, for example, in this passage from George Puttenham's *The Arte of English Poesie* (1598):

... the first and most bitter invective against vice and vicious men, was the *Satyre*: which to th' intent their bitterness should breed none ill will ... and besides to make their admonitions and reproofs seem graver and of more efficacy, they made wise as if the gods of the woods, whom they called *Satyres* or *Silvanes*, should appear and recite those verses of rebuke, whereas indeed they were but disguised persons under the shape of *Satyres*, as who would say, these terrene and base gods being conversant with mans affairs and spiers out of all their secret faults.

Satire, therefore, was a means whereby the poets masked their intentions. These 'base gods', with their knowledge of all human faults, were part goat, and consequently lecherous and malicious, and the 'satyre' to which they lent their name dealt with the baser elements of human experience, 'wars and lechery'. So what we see here is that in so far as the term 'satire' refers to a literary form at all, it is to one that is a flexible *satura*, but that it more properly refers to an attitude rather than a form and that is why it can be accommodated in a variety of other forms.

If we think of *Troilus and Cressida* as a play with a flexible, inclusive and, so far, indefinable form, one curious feature in the landscape of the scholarly discussion of the play's genre may strike us: in spite of the fact that the play is called a 'history' on both versions of the Quarto title-page as well as in the 1609 entry in the Stationers' Register, it has rarely been treated by critics as a history play. This may seem all the more strange when we consider that the classic statement of the world view that has been taken to underlie the Elizabethan concept of how history is ordered, the so-called 'Elizabethan world picture', is Ulysses' speech on degree. The general critical reluctance to consider the play as history may be because, as with so many other terms, there seems to have been no clear contemporary agreement about its meaning. In their categorical division of the plays for the First Folio, its editors, Heminge and Condell, rather arbitrarily applied the term 'histories' to the ten plays devoted to real English kings, including under this heading *Richard II* and *Richard III*, both of which had in Quarto editions been called tragedies. But such plays as *Julius Caesar* also dealt with history, and Shakespeare found the stories of the legendary kings Macbeth, Lear and Cymbeline in Holinshed's *Chronicle*, where he also found the stories of the historical English kings about whom he wrote. Clearly the categories of history and tragedy were not mutually exclusive and since the extant history plays are formally rather a diverse group it appears that the term 'history' – like the term 'satire' – refers not to a form, but to a particular perspective on the material it contains.

Elizabethan historiographers were not so much concerned with establishing the factual details of events (which in any case is very difficult to do, as contemporary historians, with their far more sophisticated methods, are well aware) as with finding in them parallels that could be used to present a model that would teach an oblique lesson to contemporary rulers by showing, for example, the dangers of tyranny. History plays performed a similar function, providing, in effect, a political commentary. As we have already seen, the story of the disorder that brought about the downfall of Troy contained disturbing parallels with the uncertain times in which men lived at the end of Elizabeth's reign; seen in this light, and in view of the lengthy tradition in which the story of Brutus had made Troy a part of English history, *Troilus and Cressida* might well have been intended as a history play.

But none of this is conclusive and in the end we have to see the play as a kind of hybrid, containing within itself opposing elements and resisting any attempt to confine it to a particular category. This may not be a bad thing, for critical inquiry has often been vitiated by attempts to insist on the unitary nature of works of art. Dryden's characterization of the play as a tragedy that does not fulfil the requirements of tragedy means that the play must be counted a failure in his terms. But the truth may rather be that, trapped by his own terminology, Dryden disabled himself from understanding what Shakespeare was actually doing, as his extensive re-writing of the play suggests. If we are to understand *Troilus and Cressida* we must not fall into the same error, but must accept the play on its own terms. It does indeed include much that is tragic, but also much that is comic, and it generates irony and a satiric vision by allowing the tragic and the comic to interrogate each other. Its events are seen from many perspectives, some of them contradictory, and we do it no service by insisting that any one of these perspectives offers the 'correct' way of reading the play.

Structure

The conclusion of either a comedy or a tragedy usually gives us a sense of completion or closure. When in *Twelfth Night* Viola can finally reveal herself to Orsino as his ideal wife, we feel that this is a satisfying resolution to the action of the play. So also when Hamlet in the process of destroying his corrupt enemy brings about his own death; the pattern that the play has developed has come to a point of equilibrium that we call an ending. Of course, that ending may suggest that something else is about to begin, a happy marriage, or a new regime; and even if, as some critics do, we feel that these endings are ambiguous (Orsino is in no way good enough to be Viola's husband; there are reasons to doubt the ability of Fortinbras to create a better Denmark), the very *form* of the play makes us feel that we have come to a point of rest. Satirical comedy also gives us something of this sense when it achieves the exposure of its victims, even though we may be aware that they will not be changed for the better by this exposure. But *Troilus and Cressida* allows us no such sense of completion. At the end of the play Cressida has gone off into a future about which the play gives us hardly a hint, and Troilus, enraged by the loss of Cressida and of Hector, is preparing to go on fighting. The end of Troy is, of course, implied by the death of Hector, as Agamemnon states:

> If in his death the gods have us befriended,
> Great Troy is ours, and our sharp wars are ended.
>
> (V.9.9–10)

But that end is achieved in history, not in the play; *Troilus and Cressida* resists closure of a more formal sort.

The structure of *Troilus and Cressida* is not, therefore, formally controlled by the ending to which it leads (except in so far as its inconclusive conclusion reflects the ambiguous tensions of the play itself). It is developed, rather, through the principle of simultaneity already mentioned, constantly presenting antithetical possibilities through juxtapositions, argument and conflict. The most obvious antitheses within the structure arise from the struggle between Greeks and Trojans, but there are also antitheses that develop out of the parallel presentation of the two plots, which concern the private and the public issues of war. They have equal weight, the priority (implied by the play's title) of the love-plot being questioned by the foregrounding of the war-plot in the Prologue. The two levels of action run parallel to one another until they merge, and they are connected thematically by the fact that they both show men motivated by excessive desire (or 'will', or 'appetite' as it is termed in the play), and structurally by the pivotal figure of Troilus. The war-plot raises questions about the ends of war, how they are to be achieved, and how they are to be judged worthy, testing theoretical and idealistic attitudes against political necessity and the painful reality of war. The love-plot also tests idealism, presenting it as self-delusion that either confirms itself or shatters against the reality of the 'other'. Each of the two plots is moved along by a manipulator (Ulysses in the one, Pandarus in the other) whose work is defeated by events, and together they take Troy and Troilus from the illusion of success to a confrontation with reality and to the verge of inevitable annihilation.

The controlling principle of simultaneity, of 'is-and-is-not', is put into effect in part by juxtapositions and contrasts, so that actions taking place at any one moment cast an ironic, usually deflationary light on what has preceded them, and will themselves be subjected to a similar interrogation by what follows. Thus the audience is constantly being invited to question and revise its judgements. The opening of the play presents an excellent example of this structural technique: the Prologue is spoken by an armed soldier who, in an introduction appropriate to a

21

play that is to be about heroic actions, talks of the conditions of the Trojan War. However, the anticipation set up in the audience by this martial Prologue is immediately disappointed when, in the play's first scene, the titular hero Troilus enters and demands most unheroically to be unarmed because the turmoil in his heart has deprived him of the will to fight. During this scene the idealistic Troilus sets up Cressida as a worthy object of his love, but the romantic elevation of his feelings, upon which he insists, is put into question by the prosaic commentary of Pandarus, and in the scene following this we meet a defiantly flesh-and-blood Cressida who is not by any means the Cressida he has imagined.

The parallel that can be drawn between the roles of Ulysses and Pandarus as manipulators within the two plots indicates another way in which situations and perspectives can be seen to comment on one another. Characters are linked through sets of analogies, recurrent motifs and visual parallels that operate throughout the larger structure of the play. The implications suggested by the structural linking of Pandarus with Ulysses cast an ironic light on the motives of the latter. Agamemnon and Paris are linked as ineffectual authority-figures. The pride of Achilles is mocked in the emulous figure of Ajax. The visual motif of the soldier disarmed by a woman moves from Troilus to Paris to Hector, and finally to Achilles, but is linked also to the image of the disarmed Hector murdered by Achilles who had earlier expressed 'a woman's longing' to see him. Cressida is linked to Helen through frequent comparisons made by Pandarus, through the materialistic ways in which both women are valued, and by becoming the object of opposed Greek and Trojan lovers; but she is also linked by a visual analogy to Cassandra, the figure of feminine powerlessness who bursts in on the Trojan debate 'raving, with her hair about her ears' when her own powerlessness in a masculine world brings her to a similar state: 'Tear my bright hair, and scratch my praised cheeks; /Crack my clear voice with sobs' (IV.2.106–7).

What are we to make of this complexity of perspectives, these conflicting images? In the Prologue itself Shakespeare seems to mock his audience for the difficulties that he knows the play is going to create. Very few of his plays have prologues, but in those that do he generally asks for the good opinion of the audience, as for example in *Romeo and Juliet*, where those present are asked to listen 'with patient ears', or in *Henry V*, written shortly before *Troilus and Cressida*, where the Prologue begs the audience 'gently to hear, kindly to judge'. The present Prologue, however, makes no such modest request; it hardly seems to expect or care about the audience's good opinion, but rather defies us to like the play:

> Like or find fault; do as your pleasures are;
> Now good or bad, 'tis but the chance of war.
> (30–31)

It is a challenge, and its tone prepares us well for the much greater challenge of the play that is to follow.

Properly to appreciate the effect of constant dislocation, a reading of *Troilus and Cressida* should keep in mind the essential swiftness of the play's construction (which contrasts with the peculiar lassitude of the action in which much is said but very little happens), something that would be brought out in a good performance. Although modern editions of the play divide it into five acts, none of the early editions has these act divisions; they were imposed on the play by later editors. To feel the rhythm of the play, therefore, it is helpful to ignore the pauses implied by these divisions and think of it in terms of continuous forward movement. For example, the railing of Thersites against Agamemnon in II.1 will clearly be fully effective only if Thersites bursts on to the stage immediately on the departure of the Greek leaders in I.3. The one point in the play where a break seems appropriate comes not at the end of an act, but between I I I.2 and I I I.3, after the union of Troilus and Cressida, and before Calchas makes his request to the Greeks that will drive the play in a new direction, although even here one may feel that the close juxtaposition of the two scenes would underscore the irony and futility of the lovers' prayers and vows of constancy.

The action of the play takes place in three main locales: Priam's palace, Cressida's house and the Greek camp. Within these locales there are subsidiary locations: the chambers of Troilus and Paris, for example, and the royal council chamber in Troy on the one hand, the tents of various Greek leaders on the other. These different locations would have been identified by simple properties; the Elizabethan theatre did not make use of the kind of elaborate or realistic scenery that we are familiar with today. The events are spread over some three days. At the end of the opening scene Troilus and Aeneas go off to fight, and in the following scene Cressida and Pandarus watch them and the other warriors return, presumably in the afternoon. The Greek debate takes place that evening (although it should be noted that while in I.3.262 Aeneas refers to 'this dull and long-continued truce' there is no other reason to believe that a gap is intended between the first two scenes and the rest of the play), and Aeneas interrupts it with Hector's challenge for a fight on the following morning. Aeneas does not attend the Trojan debate, which presumably goes on while he is away. Troilus and Cressida are brought together that night, and the exchange between Cressida and Antenor is effected on the following morning. The Trojans attend the Greek camp shortly after, and the fight between Hector and Ajax takes place later that day. The feasting that follows goes on into the night, and it is dark when Troilus witnesses Cressida's infidelity. The final battle takes place on the third day, ending as night falls.

Troilus and Cressida

What follows is an account of the play's structure. It is not intended as a plot summary, but is rather an attempt to trace the way in which *Troilus and Cressida* develops its meanings through analogies, contrasts and dislocations, subjecting all positions to a deflating scrutiny through the ironic interplay of attitudes. The act and scene divisions are used as a matter of convenience for purposes of reference, but the reader is asked to think of the play as a continuous forward flow.

Prologue

The 'Prologue armed' functions in a very illuminating way as an example of the larger structural method of the play. A dramatic prologue usually provides the expository background that leads the audience from the 'real' world into the fictional 'play' world. This Prologue does that: it gives an account of the events that brought the Greeks to the point of exhaustion before the walls of Troy, at which the play begins. It does something else, however, that is rather more interesting. It undermines certain expectations that the audience must have brought into the theatre from outside, for, drawn to the theatre by an advertisement that gave it, presumably, a description of the play something like that of the Quarto title-page, the audience will have come to see a dramatization of the well-known love-story of Troilus and Cressida. No mention, however, is made of the famed lovers: the Prologue speaks only of the Trojan War.

In his account of the events that brought the Greeks to Troy, the Prologue provides a further disturbance of expectations. The story he tells is couched in an elevated, portentous, highly Latinate style:

> From isles of Greece
> The princes orgulous, their high blood chafed,
> Have to the port of Athens sent their ships
> Fraught with the ministers and instruments
> Of cruel war. Sixty and nine that wore
> Their crownets regal from th'Athenian bay

Put forth toward Phrygia, and their vow is made
To ransack Troy, within whose strong immures
The ravished Helen, Menelaus' queen,
With wanton Paris sleeps – and that's the quarrel.

(1–10)

The high style is appropriate for the serious events outlined here, but in the first of many dislocations in the play the Prologue deflates his own rhetoric, interrupting its rhythms with four words, 'and that's the quarrel', their flat matter-of-factness indicating the mundane reality of the pretext that has brought these sixty and nine princes orgulous to Troy. The effect is to present opposing perspectives: the high idealism and belief in honour that has brought the Greeks to Troy is held up for scrutiny against a much more sceptical attitude that renders the mighty heroic conflict into a mere quarrel. This will be one of the major incongruities of the play.

Act I, Scenes 1 and 2

The first two scenes introduce the love-plot, gaining their main effect from the contrast they present between the real Cressida and the idea of her that Troilus has generated, an idea that causes the first major dislocation of the play when Troilus enters, armed like the Prologue, but demanding to be unarmed because the torments of what he sees as unattainable love have taken away his will to fight. Through his participation in the two plots Troilus is the play's main unifying device, and his opening lines indicate one way in which the two plots reflect one another:

Why should I war without the walls of Troy,
That find such cruel battle here within?
Each Trojan that is master of his heart,
Let him to field; Troilus, alas, hath none.

(I.1.2–5)

This martial metaphor of disturbance that defines the larger conflict serves also to describe the love-conflict, and the connection between the two is reinforced by the quibble on the word 'heart' as seat both of courage and of amatory passion: having lost his heart to Cressida, Troilus has no heart for the fight. He thus presents an image that recurs throughout the play, of a warrior disarmed by a beautiful woman, of desire overcoming duty. The weakness that makes Troilus the romantic victim of Cressida also makes him the comic victim of Pandarus, without whom he cannot reach Cressida, and the self-conscious sentiment of the lover's comparisons is put into question by the comic prose that interrupts them. Furthermore, the material nature of Pandarus' cake-baking metaphor – the first of a series of images concerned with food and its devouring – serves here (like Troilus' later image of Cressida as a pearl and himself as a merchant trying to buy her) to turn Cressida into an object, revealing the strongly materialistic obverse of Troilus' idealism. It has the effect of uncovering the erotic element that Troilus is trying to suppress from his idealization of his feelings for Cressida, and that surfaces again in the sensuality of his attempt to visualize 'Her eyes, her hair, her cheek, her gait, her voice' (I.1.55), the softness and whiteness of her hand.

The introduction of Cressida casts an ironic light on the opening scene, for it reveals how little the Cressida that Troilus imagines has to do with the real thing. She is pretty, witty, sexually knowing, and rather better able than Troilus to handle Pandarus, who is defeated in all his attempts to interest her in the young man. And yet, when she is alone, she reveals that there is, in fact, no need for Pandarus to try to make Troilus attractive to her or for Troilus to worry about unrequited love:

> But more in Troilus thousandfold I see
> Than in the glass of Pandar's praise may be.
> (I.2.284–5)

Cressida is quick-witted and, if we judge from the bawdy nature of her conversation with Pandarus, rather more sexually aware, and certainly more realistic, than Troilus. She responds to Troilus' feelings, but she also realizes the dangers inherent in her situation, and is determined to remain in control. She is well aware that any object can lose its value once it has been obtained ('Things won are done; joy's soul lies in the doing'), and she also recognizes, as Troilus does not, that his love for her may well be love of his own false image of her: 'Men prize the thing ungained more than it is.' She is more woman than girl, and is not, certainly, the girl Troilus imagines.

Act I, Scene 3 to Act II, Scene 3

These four scenes present the war-plot. Each side debates the issues of the war, and on each side we see how the values of authority and order, intelligence and reason, desirable though they are, are difficult to achieve or maintain in the face of reality. Having set up a complex and contradictory nexus of perceptions about Troilus and Cressida, Shakespeare sets up an equally complex set of attitudes to the war and its pretexts.

The Greek discussion (it is not really a debate, since no one disagrees with Ulysses) concerns the question of what should be done to win the war. The Greek leader Agamemnon states the problem at some length, though his point is not a difficult one: after seven years of fighting they are not getting anywhere, but they cannot blame themselves because their failure is due to Jupiter who is testing their constancy, and therefore they must accept their setbacks with stoical patience. He uses, however, the kind of inflated rhetoric that we have heard in the Prologue, and we might well be somewhat suspicious of him, the more so when his words are followed up by the aggrandizing speech of wise old Nestor, who does little more than paraphrase what Agamemnon has said. The point seems to be that if Agamemnon's diagnosis is true there is no answer to the problem, since there is nothing that the Greeks, as mere mortals, can do to improve their situation. He is, in effect, a leader denying (apparently without noticing it) his ability to lead.

When Ulysses begins to speak it appears that he too will be empty of ideas, since he begins with an even more extended piece of deferential rhetoric than Nestor's, and it takes him fifteen lines simply to ask to be allowed to speak. However, it becomes clear that his deference is a matter of tact rather than obsequiousness, for his own analysis of the situation, presented in his famous speech on degree, suggests that the Greek failure is in large part due to a failure of leadership: 'The specialty of rule hath been neglected' (I.3.78). This remarkable speech has often been understood as a statement of Shakespeare's own opinions, and certainly it articulates ideas that were an integral part of the official Elizabethan view of the world. However, in its dramatic context it is a very clever piece of manipulation with a clear political purpose: to shake Agamemnon out of the defeatist lethargy that has been revealed in his own speech. Successful organization, according to Ulysses, depends upon a hierarchy; if the head of the hierarchy fails in its authority, the whole world, in a kind of domino theory, will fall into chaos:

> The general's disdained
> By him one step below, he by the next,
> That next by him beneath: so every step,
> Exampled by the first pace that is sick
> Of his superior, grows to an envious fever
> Of pale and bloodless emulation . . .
>
> (I.3.129–34)

The account that Ulysses gives of the problem is brilliant, and his powerful rhetoric certainly carries along his primary audience of Greek leaders, as is demonstrated by the response of Nestor, who had previously agreed with Agamemnon but now agrees with Ulysses.

When asked by Agamemnon what the remedy for this sickness might be, Ulysses apparently evades the question, for he simply goes on to give specific examples of the general problem he has diagnosed: Achilles has got out of hand; his withdrawal from the battle is the result of his contempt for the leaders, a contempt demonstrated by his enjoyment of Patroclus' parodies of their behaviour. If Ulysses' immediate audience is carried away by his oratory, however, the theatre audience may by now be a little more sensitized to the ambiguous possibilities of rhetoric, and may wonder how it is expected to respond to the bitter condemnation of Patroclus and his mimicry:

> . . . Patroclus
> Upon a lazy bed, the livelong day
> Breaks scurril jests,
> And with ridiculous and awkward action –
> Which, slanderer, he imitation calls –
> He pageants us.
>
> (I.3.146–51)

There can be little doubt about Ulysses' hostility here to the performances of Patroclus, yet he goes on to recreate those performances in a cruel and accurate performance of his own that apparently mimics and discredits the mimicry of Patroclus, but actually mocks Agamemnon and Nestor. In effect he implicates himself, apparently in full consciousness, in the very thing he condemns.

The fundamental point made by Ulysses is that the parodists and mockers (Patroclus performing for Achilles, and, in a parody of that relationship, Thersites performing for Ajax) use their 'art' to undermine hierarchy, to deny the value of policy and to effect the dethronement of reason. Certainly he provides a powerful argument, and yet his own function as parodist here adds an element of ambiguity that may make us uneasy about giving his analysis the wholehearted acceptance he seeks. At any rate, after his rational and authoritative analysis of the failure of reason and authority in the Greek camp we do not learn what he would do to reinstate order, reason and authority, for the scene is interrupted by the arrival from Troy of Aeneas, who raises further questions about the theory of order as presented by Ulysses:

> How may
> A stranger to those most imperial looks
> Know them from eyes of other mortals?
> (I.3.223–5)

This provides an interesting commentary on the principle of hierarchy, since that principle is dependent upon the acknowledged superiority of one man over another. But in what does that superiority lie? The divine characteristics of leadership that should display themselves in imperial looks apparently do not display themselves in any obvious way in the looks of Agamemnon, since Aeneas fails to recognize him:

> Which is that god in office, guiding men?
> Which is the high and mighty Agamemnon?
> (I.3.231–2)

It is difficult to know (as Agamemnon himself notes) whether Aeneas has genuinely failed to recognize him, or whether this is an act of mockery, but in either case its effect is somewhat to deflate the Greek pretensions.

The challenge from Hector that Aeneas brings is rather out of place in the midst of this brutal war, since it offers single combat to anyone who is willing to fight with Hector over the purely chivalrous (and surely specious) question of whose lady is 'wiser, fairer, truer'. There is something unquestionably comic, even ludicrous, about this whole situation, but Agamemnon and Nestor affect to take it seriously, with the latter insisting that his lady was more beautiful than Hector's grandmother. Ulysses, however, in opportunist manner, sees in this challenge the possibility of an answer to his problem of disorder. A rigged lottery will ensure that Ajax is chosen as Hector's opponent, giving the inferior man glory that Achilles should have, thus bringing the proud warrior back into line.

This is an extremely complex scene. It gives emphasis to a speech that elevates hierarchy and order as ideals, but it presents us with an authority-figure in the person of Agamemnon, 'soul and only spirit' of the Greeks, who has presided over the disintegration of order within his army, who lacks the analytical ability to see the cause of his failure, and who clearly cannot bear the weight of the ideals he should embody. It also presents us with a relentless series of diminutions, in which Agamemnon and Nestor are brought down (or 'uncrowned') by the parodies of Patroclus as recreated by Ulysses, and Agamemnon is further uncrowned by his treatment at the hands of Aeneas. Furthermore, the reliability of Ulysses, as spokesman for these ideals, is brought into question by his own implication in the disorderly attitudes he condemns, by his use of rhetoric as a persuasive tool rather than as a means of presenting truth, and by his willingness to subvert the very order he has proclaimed as essential by elevating Ajax above Achilles.

The pretensions of leadership are seen from a radically different perspective in the scene that follows, as Thersites presents his grotesque image of Agamemnon: 'Agamemnon – how if he had boils, full, all over, generally? . . . And those boils did run? – say so – did not the general run then? Were not that a botchy core? . . . Then there would come some matter from him; I see none now' (II.1.2–9). If there is a bottom level to the hierarchy in the play, it is represented by Thersites in a perspective that absolutely denies all that Ulysses wants to uphold. And yet, in spite of the disease and ugliness that Thersites embodies, there is an undeniable intelligence there that often reveals truth, as in his demonstration of the nature of Ajax's emulous attitude to Achilles: 'Thou grumblest and railest every hour on Achilles, and thou art as full of envy at his greatness as Cerberus is at Proserpina's beauty, ay, that thou bark'st at him' (II.1.30–33).

This scene brings together Thersites and Ajax, Patroclus and Achilles, the parodists, imitators and mockers who were condemned by Ulysses and Nestor. It is strategically placed between the two debate scenes, and in its noisy violence it presents an image of disorder in contrast to the orderly attempts at discussion of those two scenes. It may be seen to imply a comment on them, however; when Achilles tries to make peace between Ajax and Thersites, his question 'What's the quarrel?' echoes the 'and that's the quarrel' of the Prologue, reminding us again of the real nature of the war that is debated in those loftier scenes.

The Trojan debate is not concerned with the practical matter of how the war is to be won, but with the ethical question of whether it should be continued at all. Priam projects a strong sense of weariness when he asks whether the Trojans should bring an end to the war, 'After so many hours, lives, speeches spent' (II.2.1.), by returning Helen. The question divides his sons, setting Hector and Helenus, as realists, against Troilus and Paris, the apparent idealists. Hector argues, first, that Helen is not worth the number of lives that have been sacrificed for her, and that no more lives should be given up on behalf of a woman who means nothing to the Trojans. Troilus replies that defending Helen is a matter that involves their father's honour; apparently he has not noticed the tone in which Priam raised the question, and also seems to have forgotten his own view on the matter as expressed in the play's opening scene:

> Fools on both sides! Helen must needs be fair,
> When with your blood you daily paint her thus.

> I cannot fight upon this argument;
> It is too starved a subject for my sword.
>
> (I.1.92–5)

When Helenus points out the irrationality of Troilus' argument the young man responds, not by showing that he *does* have reason, but first by calling Helenus a coward, then by banishing reason from any discussion of war at all:

> Nay, if we talk of reason,
> Let's shut our gates and sleep. Manhood and honour
> Should have hare-hearts, would they but fat their thoughts
> With this crammed reason; reason and respect
> Make livers pale and lustihood deject.
>
> (II.2.46–50)

Reason, in effect, is seen by Troilus to oppose what he thinks of as courage.

Hector's simple reply that Helen is not worth the lives it costs to keep her initiates a discussion of the nature of value. 'What's aught but as 'tis valued?' (II.2.53) asks Troilus, implying a purely relativist view, that nothing has value in itself, but only as it is perceived by someone who wants it – a view which, had Troilus been a more consistent character, might have protected him from his own evaluation of Cressida. Hector replies that what is valued must have some inherent worth: ''Tis mad idolatry/to make the service greater than the god' (II.2.57–8). Troilus, despite his rejection of reason, tries in response to give a reasoned argument to support his view: a choice once made must be followed through. If a man takes a wife he must stand by that choice, even if his feelings change; in the same way, we cannot give back soiled goods. When Paris first stole Helen from Menelaus the Trojan leaders applauded the act; they cannot now reject what they had once prized so highly. There is a certain amount of persuasive power in his words, but he concludes by unwittingly revealing the flaw in his own argument:

> O, theft most base,
> That we have stolen what we do fear to keep!
> But thieves unworthy of a thing so stolen,
> That in their country did them that disgrace
> We fear to warrant in our native place!
>
> (II.2.93–7)

'Theft', 'thieves', 'stolen': the moral content of these words (and Troilus' apparent blindness to it) clearly indicates the moral blindness that

31

characterizes his position. As if to underline this, Cassandra suddenly bursts in on the debate wailing her vision of the destruction of Troy, but her prophecy is dismissed by Troilus as madness.

Paris now takes over the argument, supporting what Troilus has said, and claiming that he would never retract what he has done, even if he had to defend Helen alone. When Priam points out that Paris is very much an interested party, having had all the 'honey' from the rape of Helen while others have had to suffer for it, Paris reverts to Troilus' initial argument – that keeping Helen is a matter of honour. Indeed, he goes further than Troilus, effectively elevating Helen and turning her into an ideal, a principle for whom any man would be willing to die:

> Well may we fight for her whom, we know well,
> The world's large spaces cannot parallel.
>
> (II.2.162–3)

One might feel (though Troilus does not) that having the shallow sensualist Paris agree with him undermines Troilus' argument rather than strengthens it.

Hector now concludes the debate by pointing out that Troilus and Paris have argued as young men who are too callow to discuss such weighty questions, because they let passion overwhelm judgement. He goes back to Troilus' early argument about the duties of a husband to a wife, pointing out that what it actually shows is that Helen should be returned to her rightful husband – the opposite of what Troilus took it to show. If an action is wrong, we cannot make it right by persisting in it. 'Hector's opinion/Is this in way of truth' (II.2.189–90), and by any reasonable judgement he has clearly won the debate. Yet at this point he throws his victory away:

> ... Yet, ne'ertheless,
> My sprightly brethren, I propend to you
> In resolution to keep Helen still;
> For 'tis a cause that hath no mean dependence
> Upon our joint and several dignities.
>
> (II.2.190–94)

It is an astonishing moment. Unlike Troilus and Paris, Hector believes in reason, yet he yields to the firebrand passion of his 'sprightly' brothers and opts for dignity, glory – that is, for pride. Furthermore, as he reminds us at the end of the scene, he has already sent his challenge to the Greeks, so presumably he had never had any intention of giving up Helen. His part in the argument has been a game and he abdicates his responsibility as defender of reason.

Thersites offers his cynical opinion on the issues debated by the Trojans too. He has a clear answer to the question of whether Helen is worth fighting for: 'the vengeance on the whole camp – or rather, the Neapolitan bone-ache – for that, methinks, is the curse dependent on those that war for a placket' (II.3.17–20). He also has his own version of the hierarchy that so concerns Ulysses, as he tells Patroclus: 'Agamemnon is a fool to offer to command Achilles, Achilles is a fool to be commanded of Agamemnon, Thersites is a fool to serve such a fool, and Patroclus is a fool positive' (II.3.61–4). In Thersites' vision, order itself is disorder, and his appearance here links the scene we have just witnessed with the present one: Hector has turned order into disorder by rejecting the dictates of his own reason, and Achilles' withdrawal from the battle has created the disorder that Ulysses identified in the Greek debate.

As if to emphasize the abdication of reason, Achilles will give no explanation for his withdrawal from combat, and refuses even to leave his tent to receive the delegation of leaders who come to try to persuade him to return to arms. He responds neither to the commands of Agamemnon nor to the eloquence of Ulysses, being the victim of a false pride that has so overwhelmed him that he can scarcely tolerate even himself. He has become, in the image Ulysses presents of him, as a kingdom at war with itself, an emblem of discord; as such he is an embodiment of the disease that Ulysses has diagnosed as the cause of the Greek failure:

> Possessed he is with greatness,
> And speaks not to himself but with a pride
> That quarrels at self-breath. Imagined worth
> Holds in his blood such swollen and hot discourse
> That 'twixt his mental and his active parts
> Kingdomed Achilles in commotion rages,
> And batters down himself.
>
> (II.3.168–74)

The disease is not only in Achilles, for at the end of the scene Ajax appears as a comic reflection of Achilles, being also consumed by a pride he does not recognize. It is ironic that Ulysses has to inflate the pride of Ajax in his attempt to deflate that of Achilles; he is forced by the practical realities of policy to abuse the ideals that he himself has held up as being essential.

Taken as a group, these four scenes present the war-plot in a very complex manner. We are given two scenes in which serious issues are debated, but in each case the spokesman for reason is seen as unable or unwilling to sustain the ideals he has eloquently defended. Each of the two debate scenes is followed by a scene in which the issues it has considered are seen from a satirical viewpoint, presenting the chaotic reality that reason sets itself up to control.

Act III, Scene 1

The Trojan debate involved an exhaustive discussion of the conduct of the war and the value of Helen as its pretext, and we have now had a variety of perspectives on the question. For the audience, the discussion has been somewhat abstract; not having seen Helen, we cannot judge whether or not she deserves to be elevated as an ideal. Here, however, we are given a new and compelling perspective, for we see 'the face that launched a thousand ships'. This scene functions as a bridge between the two plots, for the relationship between Helen and Paris that is the root cause of the war provides a close parallel to that between Cressida and Troilus, and Pandarus is therefore an appropriate presenter. Helen is flirtatious and essentially trivial, her conversation filled with sexual innuendo. Love here is defined as 'hot deeds' (and it is not irrelevant that in this play 'hot' and 'deeds' are words usually applied to martial rather than marital acts), which we might think of more properly as lust. Love also disarms warriors, for Paris has stayed away from the battlefield under Helen's persuasion: the man who in the debate said he would fight single-handed for Helen will not fight for Troy. We are reminded of Troilus as disarmed warrior in the opening scene, and the potency of the image is increased when Paris asks Helen to 'disarm great Hector', a request with no little irony, since Hector effectively disarmed himself on Helen's behalf when he rejected the dictates of his own reason in the debate.

Act III, Scene 2

The decadent and frankly erotic atmosphere of the foregoing scene is carried by Pandarus into this one, and inevitably colours our response to the meeting of Troilus and Cressida. There is something self-indulgent and excessive about the romantic hyperbole of Troilus' vision of himself as a lost soul praying to be translated from hell to heaven:

> I stalk about her door,
> Like a strange soul upon the Stygian banks
> Staying for waftage. O, be thou my Charon,

> And give me swift transportance to those fields
> Where I may wallow in the lily-beds
> Proposed for the deserver!
>
> (III.2.7–12)

Any attempt to see Troilus as an idealistic young man trying to express the spirituality of his feelings must be brought up short against the sensuality of the image of him wallowing in lily-beds, and be brought completely down to earth by the flat practicality of Pandarus' response: 'Walk here i' th' orchard; I'll bring her straight' (III.2.15)

Troilus is a normal youth whose longings, however much he tries to elevate them, do not differ much from those of any other healthy young man faced with what is to him the pure mystery of sexuality:

> I am giddy; expectation whirls me round.
> Th' imaginary relish is so sweet
> That it enchants my sense.
>
> (III.2.16–18)

If in his inexperience he confuses goddess with woman we can hardly blame him, and when Cressida is finally brought to him, his simple words, in contrast to his earlier imaginings, suggest a genuine depth of response: 'You have bereft me of all words, lady' (III.2.53). But there is an uneasy feeling in the scene that Troilus cannot resolve a conflict within him between fantasy and reality, a feeling which is augmented by the sense that we have of Pandarus as a stage-manager manipulating a performance:

She's making her ready; she'll come straight. You must be witty now. She does so blush, and fetches her wind so short, as if she were frayed with a sprite. I'll fetch her. It is the prettiest villain; she fetches her breath as short as a new-ta'en sparrow.

> (III.2.28–32)

Pandarus here makes it appear that Cressida is preparing to play a part, and urges Troilus to do so too. The result is that the young man employs a self-conscious rhetoric through which his individual feeling is submerged in that of a kind of universal category of 'lover':

. . . we vow to weep seas, live in fire, eat rocks, tame tigers; thinking it harder for our mistress to devise imposition enough than for us to undergo any difficulty imposed. This is the monstruosity in love, lady, that the will is infinite, and the execution confined; that the desire is boundless, and the act a slave to limit.

> (III.2.75–81)

Cressida on the other hand is beset by doubts, in part about the sincerity of Troilus' feelings, in part about the wisdom of her revelation of her feelings for him. The climax of the scene comes with their joyous proclamation of their sincerity, but its strong affirmation is undercut by the ending, when the three characters step beyond the boundaries of the play and ironically predict their future reputations: 'Let all constant men be Troiluses, all false women Cressids, and all brokers-between Pandars!' (III.2.200–202). The scene pushes us in conflicting directions, for we are caught up by their excitement at the same time as we are reminded of its futility.

Act III, Scene 3

In an immediate underlining of that futility, the joy of the lovers is shown to be doomed as the traitor Calchas asks the Greeks to have him reunited with his daughter Cressida (in exchange for Antenor, who, as an audience familiar with the story would have known, will also eventually betray Troy). Diomedes, in a moment notable for its dramatic unobtrusiveness, is sent to effect the exchange. Calchas' speech is important, for it is about betrayal, and its location gives it a good deal of emphasis as it comes at the mid-point of the play, after what is the most natural place for a break, and by providing the cause for the separation of the lovers it moves the action in a new direction.

In his second attempt to bring Achilles back into the war Ulysses once more finds his position as spokesman for the correct order of things compromised when, in the interests of practical necessity, he is again forced to use deception by orchestrating the performance of the Greek leaders. In an effort to reflect Achilles' pride to him they treat him as a stranger, as he has 'estranged' himself. This is a prologue to the lengthy conversation between Ulysses and Achilles in which Ulysses talks of the fragility of reputation and its vulnerability to the destructive power of time. Achilles has become inactive because he thinks his past deeds are sufficient to allow him present glory, but Ulysses argues that deeds only have value if others applaud them, and they applaud only what is present and dynamic. If the superior man becomes passive, as Achilles has done, he risks the forfeit of his rewards to the inferior man:

> Then marvel not, thou great and complete man,
> That all the Greeks begin to worship Ajax,
> Since things in motion sooner catch the eye
> Than what stirs not.
>
> (III.3.181–4)

Again Ulysses is using his rhetorical skills for political ends rather than in the interests of truth; he is, furthermore, contradicting his own earlier argument about order, for there he was spokesman for absolute values, while here he is taking a position akin to that of Troilus in the Trojan debate: that the value of an object is purely relative, being imposed on it by the valuer.

Ajax, of course, is absurd, as is plainly illustrated by Thersites' description of him later in the scene: 'Why, he'll answer nobody, he professes not answering; speaking is for beggars; he wears his tongue in's arms' (III.3.268–70). He is one of the thousand sons of emulation, puffed up with pride; Ulysses presents him as such to Achilles, and Thersites mimics him as such. But he also reflects the absurdity of what he emulates so that his pride is precisely that of Achilles, and when, in a superb complication of perspectives, Thersites presents his 'pageant of Ajax', it is a parody of a parody of an attitude that is itself ridiculous. Furthermore, Thersites' own comic drama of Ajax has a greater effect on Achilles than the more elaborate play put on by Ulysses, so that his dramatic production is an unwitting parody of that of Ulysses. However, Achilles' intelligence is not sufficient to allow him to draw the appropriate conclusions from what he has seen, and he is left only with vague misgivings:

> My mind is troubled, like a fountain stirred,
> And I myself see not the bottom of it.
>
> (III.3.308–9)

Act IV, Scenes 1 to 4

These four scenes, set in Troy, bring the two plots together with the destructive intrusion of reality upon Troilus and Cressida in the shape of Diomedes. The black good humour of his exchanges with Aeneas provides an interesting light on the martial exchanges to come, as each of the two men admires the other as a valiant man and therefore as an enemy worthy of being killed. This is a situation that can only be considered in terms of paradox or oxymoron:

> This is the most despiteful'st gentle greeting,
> The noblest hateful love, that e'er I heard of.
>
> (IV.1.33–4)

That war should make two such men enemies is one of the terrible truths of the play, and the insufficiency of Helen as cause of the war is brought to the fore again when Paris foolishly asks whether he or Menelaus deserves her the more; cuckold and lecher both deserve her equally, is the reply, since both want her despite her soilure and dishonour:

> Both merits poised, each weighs nor less nor more;
> But he as you, each heavier for a whore.
>
> (IV.1.66–7)

This is a very rough answer to the question the Trojans had debated, as is Diomedes' opinion about Helen as an object not worth fighting for:

> She's bitter to her country. Hear me, Paris:
> For every false drop in her bawdy veins
> A Grecian's life hath sunk; for every scruple
> Of her contaminated carrion weight
> A Trojan hath been slain.
>
> (IV.1.69–73)

Diomedes' cynical contempt may seem excessive, but it gains greater point as it is a clear echo of Troilus' opinion on the question at the opening of the play (I.1.92–5), an opinion now tragically (for Troy) abandoned.

Troilus and Cressida awaken from their night of love unaware of the impending disaster, though there is a curious unease about their awakening. Troilus shows tender concern for Cressida: 'To bed, to bed. Sleep kill those pretty eyes' (IV.2.4), but his concern appears rather like an anxiety to be going; it certainly worries Cressida, who fears he is weary of her now that he has had what he wanted from her:

> Prithee, tarry –
> You men will never tarry –
> O foolish Cressid, I might have still held off,
> And then you would have tarried!
>
> (IV.2.15–18)

Strange also is his silence at Pandarus' smutty suggestiveness – hardly the response of a protective romantic lover. And when Aeneas informs him of the proposed exchange of Cressida for Antenor he has almost nothing to say beyond asking Aeneas not to mention his presence in Cressida's house, in contrast to the passionate resistance of Cressida herself. The violence of her language (IV.2.95–108) makes Troilus' words to Paris seem artificial and self-conscious:

> I'll bring her to the Grecian presently;
> And to his hand when I deliver her,
> Think it an altar, and thy brother Troilus
> A priest, there offering to it his own heart.
>
> (IV.3.6–9)

Troilus seems to stand at some distance from his feelings; the positions of the two lovers have been reversed, with Troilus now reticent and Cressida aggressive. This is well illustrated by a comparison of Cressida's speech (IV.4.2–10) with that of Troilus (IV.4.23–6). While there is a fierce energy behind her words, he is still employing the self-conscious rhetoric of the courtly lover.

His attitude changes when Cressida pictures herself as 'A woeful Cressid 'mongst the merry Greeks' (IV.4.55), and he suddenly realizes that she will be the object of all sorts of temptations. He begins to express doubts about her ability to withstand these temptations and be true to him (doubts which he tries to elevate as 'a kind of godly jealousy', but which are just plain, ordinary human jealousy). He compares himself unfavourably with the Greeks (as he did in the opening scene of the play), and no doubt sets up an anticipation of the very temptation that he is trying to warn her against. Cressida is, quite reasonably, annoyed by these doubts about her ability to be constant, which become the more offensive when set beside his rather smug insistence on his own inability to be anything but constant (IV.4.101–7). The high strain of Troilus' pose is mocked by the entry of Diomedes who, far from being a Greek 'full of quality' of the refined sort Troilus has imagined, is supremely earthy in his attitude to Cressida.

Act IV, Scene 5

The approach to the combat between Hector and Ajax has led us to expect some sort of climax in this scene, but it develops in terms of anti-climax. The first comes immediately, when the Greek trumpet blows its summons to Hector, and is answered by the arrival of Cressida. In another little drama Ulysses orchestrates her humiliation by causing her to be kissed by each of the Greek leaders, and the 'quick sense' she shows when she eventually regains composure he then interprets, in a speech which has presented the definitive picture of Cressida to posterity, as a sign of her wantonness (IV.5.54–63). But with the immediate entry of the Trojans the scene goes on to demonstrate that, since any interpretation of character is coloured by the attitudes of the interpreter, none can be definitive: we are presented with a conflict of interpretation when the sneering Achilles remarks on Hector's pride, and Aeneas re-defines this pride as valour. We may, therefore, consider with some scepticism Ulysses' description of Troilus (IV.5. 96–112), particularly as he admits to receiving it at second hand from Aeneas.

The ensuing fight between Hector and Ajax provides another anti-climax, when they agree to terminate it because of their blood-relationship. We may wonder why this relationship did not prevent them from fighting at all, but perhaps Hector is not interested in the fight, since his challenge was intended for Achilles. The strength of Hector's courtesy, so strongly defended by Aeneas, is tested when he is introduced to the Greek leaders; it barely operates when he meets Menelaus, and is lost altogether under the taunting of Achilles. His encounter with Hector makes Achilles agree to re-enter the war, however. The scene ends with the preparation for Troilus' grand disillusionment when he asks Ulysses to take him to Calchas' tent.

Act V, Scene 1

Achilles is now worked up to kill Hector, and it appears that the climactic confrontation for which we have been waiting will soon take place; but our anticipation is again thwarted by anti-climax when Thersites arrives with a letter from the Trojan Queen Hecuba begging Achilles not to fight, in accordance with the oath he made to her daughter Polyxena. The fundamental ignobility of Achilles is seen in his attitude to Hector, the confusion of his values in his elevation of his oath to a Trojan woman over his duty to the Greeks. Thersites' reductive commentary on the implied homosexual relationship between Achilles and Patroclus, offensive as it is, further indicates this sense of confusion, of the drowning of brain in blood. As the scene ends the leaders go off to their uneasy feast, and Thersites follows Diomedes to the assignation that is to shatter Troilus. Any doubts we may have about what Troilus is going to see are removed by Thersites' description of the 'false-hearted rogue' and 'most unjust knave' Diomedes.

Act V, Scene 2

All the issues of illusion and meaning, of knowledge and self-delusion, of observation and interpretation, that have made up so much of the argument of the play are brought together in this highly complex, theatrical scene. The assignation between Cressida and Diomedes is the object of various levels of informed and uninformed observation, and Troilus' reaction to it is itself the object of incredulous commentary by Ulysses and satirical commentary by Thersites. The audience is allowed a position of privilege, being able to impose its own interpretation upon all the others. The meeting between Cressida and Diomedes must seem a gross parody of the earlier meeting between Troilus and Cressida, with Cressida now taking the active part of wooer and Diomedes using a pretended reluctance in order to control her. Calchas has the role of go-between earlier played by Pandarus. Troilus is finally confronted with a version of Cressida that is the complete antithesis of his own. It is only the evening of the day of their parting, yet she has already learnt to speak to Diomedes in tones of intimacy; he is her 'sweet guardian', her 'sweet honey Greek'.

There are indications here of some misgivings on Cressida's part: her sudden reluctance when she gives Diomedes the sleeve that Troilus gave her is the effect of a surge of guilt at her memory of Troilus, though Diomedes thinks she is playing with him. Nevertheless, her vulnerability guarantees her defeat, and although we can sympathize with her because as victim of the war she has been turned into an object, there is nothing much to generate sympathy for her in the manner in which she blames her fall to Diomedes upon a general weakness in all women:

> Troilus, farewell! One eye yet looks on thee,
> But with my heart the other eye doth see.
> Ah, poor our sex! This fault in us I find,
> The error of our eye directs our mind;
> What error leads must err – O, then conclude,
> Minds swayed by eyes are full of turpitude.
>
> (V.2.109–114)

Troilus struggles to give a meaning to what he has witnessed, but he cannot reconcile the opposing pressures of his head and his heart except by attempting to deny what he has seen, by making this into some other Cressida, independent of his own:

> This she? No, this is Diomed's Cressida.
> If beauty hath a soul, this is not she;
> If souls guide vows, if vows are sanctimony,
> If sanctimony be the gods' delight,
> If there be rule in unity itself,
> This is not she. O madness of discourse,
> That cause sets up with and against itself!
> Bifold authority, where reason can revolt
> Without perdition, and loss assume all reason
> Without revolt. This is, and is not, Cressid!
>
> (V.2.140–49)

Of course, this *is* Cressida, but by dividing her into two Troilus avoids any admission of complicity in the illusion he created for himself, and

41

consequently experiences no enlightenment, tragic or otherwise. Instead, he moves from one form of irrationality to another, turning his passion for Cressida into a burning hatred of Diomedes.

Act V, Scene 3

The motif of a warrior disarmed by the love of a woman has recurred throughout the play from its very opening, with the images of Troilus disarmed by Cressida, of Paris disarmed by Helen, of Hector disarmed by Helen, and of Achilles disarmed by Polyxena. Here we have an ironic reversal of that image as Hector refuses to listen to Andromache, to whom as husband he owes a real duty, because of his honour, represented by the oath he has sworn to meet Achilles. His refusal to be held back deprives him of the authority to keep the enraged Troilus from the battle, and Troilus responds to his persuasions with something very close to contempt: Hector is merciful, and that is a vice in war, where there should be no place for pity. Hector considers this savage, but Troilus will no more be held back by the pleas of Hector than Hector will listen to the concerted pleas of Andromache, Cassandra and Priam. Reason has now left both of them, Hector being concerned only with reputation and Troilus completely lost in rage, which is only increased when Pandarus brings him a letter from Cressida that he knows to be words without matter.

Act V, Scenes 4 to 10

The remainder of the play deals with the various reversals of the battle, piling irony upon irony. The complete confusion that has overtaken Troilus in his single-minded pursuit of Diomedes is illustrated when, after Diomedes captures his horse, Troilus makes that rather than Cressida the motive for his hatred:

> O traitor Diomed! Turn thy false face, thou traitor,
> And pay thy life thou owest me for my horse!
>
> (V.6.6–7)

Hector's first attempt to find an enemy of 'blood and honour' gives him only the 'very filthy rogue' Thersites. He next meets Achilles (brought into the battle, not as a result of the elaborate manipulations of Ulysses, but of the death of Patroclus), but shows his 'vice of mercy' because Achilles is tired; Hector goes instead to pursue, not honour, but a Greek in sumptuous armour whom – in an act hardly reflective of courtesy – he hunts like a beast. Thersites meets Margarelon and, proclaiming himself coward and bastard, makes his departure from the battlefield and from the play.

The climax of the war-plot is the death of Hector. Having killed the knight he pursued, he has found the sumptuous armour to contain nothing but a 'most putrefied core' (an image that could stand as a metaphor for the play itself, with its relentless probing of the squalid reality often to be found beneath a fair exterior). Hector feels he has done a good day's work. He rests and, having refused to take off his arms in the right place, he now does so in precisely the wrong place and comes unarmed to an inglorious end through an inglorious act, murdered by Achilles and his Myrmidons, as if in demonstration of the validity of Troilus' savage dismissal of mercy. Achilles' own lack of mercy and the manner in which he mocks his victim turn him into a sinister monster, and he refuses to show any recognition of Hector's value or to allow him to die with dignity:

> Look, Hector, how the sun begins to set,
> How ugly night comes breathing at his heels;
> Even with the vail and dark'ning of the sun
> To close the day up, Hector's life is done.
>
> (V.8.5–8)

It is a futile ending for the hero, and its circumstances deprive it of any real possibility of tragic feeling.

It also provides an inconclusive ending to the play. The death of Hector is the necessary condition for the fall of Troy and it signifies to the Greeks that the end of Troy is imminent, but that end is outside the play, still three years in the future. Troilus, who has almost the final words of the play, also recognizes the inevitability of the end of Troy:

> Sit, gods, upon your thrones, and smile at Troy!
> I say, at once let your brief plagues be mercy,
> And linger not our sure destructions on!
>
> (V.10.7–9)

But there is nothing for him now but to go on burning up his fury, and he sets himself against gods and men, attempting to conceal in the tortured rhetoric of his verse the futility of any further struggle now that Hector is dead:

> You vile abominable tents,
> Thus proudly pight upon our Phrygian plains,
> Let Titan rise as early as he dare,

43

> I'll through and through you! – And, thou great-sized coward,
> No space of earth shall sunder our two hates;
> I'll haunt thee like a wicked conscience still,
> That mouldeth goblins swift as frenzy's thoughts. –
> Strike a free march to Troy! With comfort go;
> Hope of revenge shall hide our inward woe.

(V.10.23–31)

If we accept that Pandarus' epilogue was not intended to be cut, however, the last words of the play are given to its chief comic character. He is dismissed by Troilus in a kind of coda in which, in the tones we expect of him, he blames the world for his sufferings:

O world, world, world! Thus is the poor agent despised! O traitors and bawds, how earnestly are you set a-work, and how ill requited! Why should our endeavour be so desired, and the performance so loathed?

(V.10.36–40)

He turns from self-pity to aggression when he offers his diseases to the audience:

> Till then I'll sweat, and seek about for eases,
> And at that time bequeath you my diseases.
> (V.10.56–7)

There is a jeering harshness to this that we associate with Thersites rather than Pandarus, so that the play sends us away with a final impression that mixes the comic and the satiric and undercuts any tragic feeling that may be implied in the death of Hector.

4. Character and Idea

The question of what constitutes dramatic character is a vexed one, but it should be immediately noted that a character in a play is not fixed and cannot be completely and definitively described. In any character there is space for interpretation on the part either of the actor or of the reader, and differing interpretations will produce different accounts of a character. For example, it is possible to produce a reading of Troilus that presents him as the idealistic victim of a shallow woman, a hero who genuinely suffers through his experience and moves the play towards the tragic. It is also possible to present him as a self-deluded fool, the comic victim of his own inability to see the world as it is. Neither of these versions is true in any absolute sense; the play can support either reading (as well as other possibilities), but this depends upon an interpretation not only of the character, but also of the context, the larger network of characters and actions in which he functions within the play. That context may be further enlarged by a number of external factors. The most obvious one in the case of *Troilus and Cressida* is the fact that the characters do not exist only in the play; they have a 'history' outside the play that must affect to some degree not only what the dramatist can do with them but also how the audience will respond to them.

By taking a story as well known as this one, Shakespeare was limiting himself in certain ways. Some aspects of the characters were prescribed. He was bound to keep to their broad outlines as he found them in his sources, as well as to the larger patterns of their experiences. Within those broad outlines, however, he was able to allow himself some flexibility in dealing with motivation and response, and so to provide a new perspective from which the characters could be seen. This meant that a whole set of responses were developed from outside the play, as the audience tested Shakespeare's characters against expectations brought from their knowledge of the characters in other contexts. Shakespeare used the fact that his audience would have anticipated a Troilus like the ideal courtly lover of medieval tradition to generate tensions that would affect their judgement of the much more ambiguous Troilus of his play. In the same way, his Cressida is doomed by her pre-history as the embodiment of feminine perfidy, and yet much of the interest of her character comes from her struggle against this very archetype. A dramatic character, therefore, is perhaps best understood as fluid rather than fixed, a complex of impulses and attitudes that is worked upon by other complexes of impulses and attitudes, both in the play (other characters) and outside it (the audience or the reader).

A dramatic character can be presented in a limited number of ways: through what he says, through what he does, and through the way other characters react to him and what they say about him. None of these ways is simple. There are always inconsistencies in a character's presentation of himself, which are the very things that give him complexity; there may be a distance between what he says and what he does, or between what he says at one moment and what he says at another, and the meaning of the character will depend upon how that distance is interpreted. Similarly, what other characters say about him must be understood in the light of the fact that they are not infallible, but are themselves fluid complexes of impulses and attitudes, and are themselves open to interpretation. Each of the characters in *Troilus and Cressida* has a vision of the world that is limited, but that he takes to be true; this limits the ability to judge, so that the problem of how a character is to be understood is not just a problem for the audience, it is actually one of the major issues of the play itself. For example, in IV.5 there is a brief description of Diomedes by Ulysses:

> 'Tis he; I ken the manner of his gait.
> He rises on the toe; that spirit of his
> In aspiration lifts him from the earth.
> (IV.5.14–16)

Ulysses reads Diomedes through an external action: the way he walks indicates what kind of man he is, and the connection that Ulysses makes seems to express strong approval of Diomedes, suggesting a lofty spirit, a man who strives to raise himself above the earthly or material. At the end of V.1 we are given a rather lengthier account of Diomedes, this time by Thersites:

> That same Diomed's a false-hearted rogue, a most unjust knave; I will no more trust him when he leers than I will a serpent when he hisses. He will spend his mouth, and promise, like Brabbler the hound; but when he performs, astronomers foretell it, that it is prodigious, there will come some change. The sun borrows of the moon when Diomed keeps his word.
> (V.1.84–91)

It is difficult to see how these two descriptions can refer to the same man, and our first impulse might well be to accept that of Ulysses, who is so often set up as the exemplar of wisdom and clear-sightedness in the play, rather than that of Thersites, who, being a 'core of envy', can hardly be expected to give a balanced view. And yet we may feel that our own experience of Diomedes, with his aggressive arrogance and his cynical exploitation of Cressida, is closer to the image presented by Thersites than to that presented by Ulysses. We are left with a riddle: not only do we not know what Diomedes 'really' is, but we must also modify our view of the relative reliability of Ulysses and Thersites.

This is an important consideration in the case of our response to Ulysses since he provides a number of apparently authoritative characterizations of others, most notably of Troilus and Cressida. He it is who defines Cressida as a daughter of the game, and his lengthy description of Troilus (IV.5.96–109) draws attention to itself because of the prominent position it occupies, immediately before the combat between Hector and Ajax. As we shall see, however, his characterizations are not to be accepted without question. They reveal his preoccupation (one shared by many of the characters) with the slippery problems involved in trying to fix and reveal the nature of others. Such character description may seem, at first sight, to give a precise image of what it attempts to present, but it is not to be trusted. Indeed, the most striking thing about it is the perceivable distance between what is presented as 'truth' about a character, and what we ourselves are shown of that character. A good example of this comes in I.2, with Alexander's sketch of Ajax:

> This man, lady, hath robbed many beasts of their particular additions: he is valiant as the lion, churlish as the bear, slow as the elephant; a man into whom nature hath so crowded humours that his valour is crushed into folly, his folly sauced with discretion. There is no man hath a virtue that he hath not a glimpse of, nor any man an attaint but he carries some stain of it. He is melancholy without cause, and merry against the hair; he hath the joints of everything, but everything so out of joint that he is a gouty Briareus, many hands and no use, or purblind Argus, all eyes and no sight.

(I.2.19–30)

Once again we see how the play functions in terms of the idea of simultaneity. This is, and is not Ajax. The animal similes have a certain appropriateness: he is churlish and slow. But little else in Alexander's characterization applies to the Ajax that we see in the play. And so it is with all the frequent character definitions in this play: they are, and are not true.

This problem of how another individual can be apprehended or what it means to know another (or, for that matter, what it means to know one's self) is one of the main preoccupations of *Troilus and Cressida*.

False judgement of the self leads to misjudgement of others, and there is a constant concern with how to read, how to interpret. The slippery question of the relationship between appearance and essence, between illusion and reality, between word and thing, between rhetoric and content, concerns virtually all the characters in the play. What is worth seeking, what is worth fighting for, how to judge its value – these are questions that are scrutinized from a wealth of conflicting positions, but there are no privileged positions, and finally no satisfactory answers. Troilus wants to believe in love, honour and truth, but locates them in the wrong place. Cressida wants to be something better than she is, but is finally too weak to be anything more than herself. Ulysses believes in order and the power of intelligence, but is constantly frustrated by practical necessity. Hector too believes in right reason, but discards the promptings of his own reason because reputation is more important. All are mocked by Thersites, who can find no value anywhere, not even in himself. What follows is an attempt to locate the major characters within this complex of attitudes.

Greeks and Trojans

Because it dramatizes the contention between two opposing armies, *Troilus and Cressida* seems at first sight to depend on an antithesis between two world views, and the prominence given to the Greek and Trojan debates encourages this impression. If we consider these world views as they are presented in the debates, the Greeks emerge as pragmatists, concerned to bring the war to a successful conclusion, and prepared to use whatever methods may be necessary, including trickery, to achieve that end; for them, the question of the value of what they are fighting for never arises. The Trojans, on the other hand, present themselves as idealists, less concerned with victory (although obviously they want to win) than with honour and reputation, and the value of what is being fought for. This structure of apparently contrasting views has led many commentators to try to demonstrate that the play itself is a kind of debate, a philosophical inquiry into the nature of honour, or reason, or idealism, and that opposing attitudes or sets of values are represented by the two sides. Furthermore, because of the contemporary and longstanding English preference for the Trojans and distrust of the Greeks, and perhaps also because of the natural tendency to sympathize with the underdog, one very influential school of critical thought argued that all the positive values of human beauty and dignity were on the Trojan side, while the Greeks represented all that was bestial and stupid. This is not a tenable position, however, because it makes a division between the two sides that is too rigid, and it ignores the strong element of criticism in the play of Trojan materialism and the failure of the Trojans to live up to the standards they proclaim. The problem with any attempt to demonstrate that the play is a debate is that no neat equilibrium can be found. On both sides the spokesman for the higher values of intelligence and moral sense fails to act in accordance with his own precepts, demonstrating the distance between what men claim is possible and what the realities of being human allow. On both sides we see men deceiving themselves about what they are and about what is to be valued.

Greeks and Trojans may in certain ways represent opposed attitudes (or, in some cases, merely strike different poses), but the play indicates also that there are fundamental similarities between them, that they share a common condition. Impelled by will or desire, deceived by illusions often of their own making, seeking some grain of meaning in a chaotic world, they are all victims of an aimless reality and the workings of time. The physical emblem of this common condition is the 'lord of Trojan blood', Ajax, son of a Greek father and the abducted Trojan Hesione:

> This Ajax is half made of Hector's blood,
> In love whereof half Hector stays at home;
> Half heart, half hand, half Hector comes to seek
> This blended knight, half Trojan and half Greek.
>
> (IV.5.83–6)

But if the image of Ajax represents the common ground that Greeks and Trojans share, it is a negative image, for he is a figure of confusion and discord, of pride, stupidity and emulation, vices of which neither Greeks nor Trojans are free.

It is not only in this emblematic aspect of Ajax that the common folly of Greeks and Trojans is implied. When Paris asks Diomedes whether he or Menelaus is the more deserving of Helen, he is, without being aware of it, asking the fundamental question about the issues of the war and the values of those who are fighting it; he expects to hear about his own superiority over Menelaus, to hear, that is, about differences, but he is told instead about similarities:

> Both alike:
> He merits well to have her, that doth seek her,
> Not making any scruple of her soilure,
> With such a hell of pain and world of charge;
> And you as well to keep her, that defend her,

> Not palating the taste of her dishonour,
> With such a costly loss of wealth and friends.
> He, like a puling cuckold, would drink up
> The lees and dregs of a flat tamed piece;
> You, like a lecher, out of whorish loins
> Are pleased to breed out your inheritors.
> Both merits poised, each weighs nor less nor more;
> But he as you, each heavier for a whore.
>
> (IV.1.55–67)

What Diomedes says here applies not just to Menelaus and Paris, for what he says about them and the value of what they are contending for implicates equally the armies that are fighting on behalf of each of them. He is speaking about the way in which both Greeks and Trojans have invested their integrity in the contest for Helen, raising a worthless woman into a 'theme of honour and renown'. Diomedes is here clear-sighted, if somewhat cynical, about the issues of the war, but he does not stand outside what he condemns, for he himself is by no means above lechery and the pursuit of a soiled woman. We are reminded that, in a clear-sighted moment of his own, Troilus anticipated Diomedes' analysis of the question, in words that could well stand as a maxim for the play: 'Fools on both sides!' Troilus, like Diomedes, is not exempt from the folly he identifies, and it is ironic that this evaluation of Helen as an object of contention should be put into the mouths of the two men who will shortly be in similar contention over Cressida. It is also characteristic of the way in which the play works that they should contravene their own most rational perceptions. Most of the play's characters are either like Troilus, falling victim to their own illusions, or like Diomedes, setting a large distance between word and deed.

Greece and Troy, like Menelaus and Paris, like Diomedes and Troilus, are in contention over the body of a woman. Whatever conclusions may be drawn about the value of that body (that is, about the issues of the Trojan debate) it is clear that the struggle has created disorder on both sides. The Greek army is a patriarchal hierarchy, dependent for its order upon each member knowing and maintaining his position within the system. As 'head and general' of the Greeks, Agamemnon has become ineffective; after seven years he has not been able to topple Troy, and the only account for this failure that he can give is the fatalistic (and ir-responsible) one that the Greeks are being tested by the gods. The wisdom that should advise authority has shrunk into the aged body of the garrulous Nestor, who seems able to offer little more than a flattering re-statement of the leader's own position. Agamemnon has lost control of his men, especially Achilles and Ajax, who are both consumed by pride, and, worse still, his authority is the subject of parody and mockery by Patroclus and Thersites. The extent of the disorder of the Greek hierarchy can be seen in the figure of Menelaus. He is King of Sparta, brother of Agamemnon, and in the Homeric story was the essential figure on whose behalf so many great Greek leaders united. Shakespeare's treatment of him is quite remarkable: Menelaus appears in six scenes, but speaks in only four of them, for a total of eleven lines, most of which are only fragments. He is present at the Greek debate but takes no part in it, speaking only once in the scene when he is sent to see who has blown a trumpet. On each of the four other occasions on which he speaks he is mocked: as a cuckold by Achilles (III.3.64), by Patroclus and Cressida (IV.5.27–44), and by the epitome of courtesy Hector (IV.5.177–80); and as a cesspool or sewer by Thersites (V.1.71–2). Having diminished the figure so ruthlessly, Shakespeare allows Thersites to complete the job by locating Menelaus at the bottom of his own bestial hierarchy (V.1.50–62). This is where disorder has left him; even Ajax is allowed more dignity.

Although it is not immediately obvious that disorder has overtaken the Trojans in the same way, they too suffer from a failure of leadership. The figure of patriarchal authority for the Trojans is Priam, but he is barely visible. He initiates the Trojan debate in a tone that implies that he is weary of the war, and his one contribution to its argument is to point out the selfish sensuality that motivates Paris in his desire to keep Helen (II.2.143–6). This would appear to indicate that he is of the same opinion as Hector when the latter is speaking for right reason; but when Hector reverses his position and embraces the firebrand arguments of Troilus, Priam has nothing to say. He fails to exert the authority he should have, as king and father, and lets his sons pursue their disastrous policy. He appears on only one other occasion, and once again fails to prevent disaster, when he adds one more ineffectual voice to the futile pleadings of Cassandra and Andromache, begging Hector not to go out to battle. His association here with the women indicates that his authority is equal to theirs, diminished to nothing.

For all Ulysses' talk of cosmic harmony, there is no real sense of providential order in the play, and when Agamemnon claims that the failure of all the Greeks' endeavours is due to a plan by the gods to test their constancy, he is simply giving a superstitious answer to a problem that he cannot understand. In the absence of any effective authority, human or divine, the characters must all struggle to find for themselves a pattern that will give meaning to their experiences, that will answer all their riddles about will and judgement, that will bring together what seems and what is. In this struggle, Greeks and Trojans are alike.

Troilus and Truth

'As true as Troilus.' The adage that the young protagonist provides for himself at the end of III.2 sums up the idea of Troilus as it had become fixed in history from the literature of the Middle Ages until the writing of Shakespeare's play. For the medieval storytellers Troilus was the great idealist, second only to Hector in virtue, courage and courtesy, and in literary tradition he became the epitome of the courtly lover, unblemished in his constancy and made to suffer as the victim of a selfish and worthless woman. But what is truth? Steadfastness in belief in a high ideal is a great virtue, but what if the object of worship is unworthy? As Hector points out, "Tis mad idolatry/To make the service greater than the god' (II.2.57–8). This is an issue central to *Troilus and Cressida*, and Shakespeare approaches his young hero with a good deal more scepticism than had any of the medieval writers.

Shakespeare's Troilus functions as the pivotal device in the play's structure, connecting the love-plot to the war-plot by his central presence in both. He is pivotal in a more fundamental way than this, however, for it is his idealism that motivates him in both plots, making him the spokesman for all 'true swains in love' in the one and the passionate advocate of honour in the other. The value of this idealism is very much open to question, however, for it is of a kind that denies the authority of reason. Its nature is made most apparent in the Trojan debate, when Troilus explicitly makes reason the antithesis of all the things he values:

> Nay, if we talk of reason,
> Let's shut our gates and sleep. Manhood and honour
> Should have hare-hearts, would they but fat their thoughts
> With this crammed reason; reason and respect
> Make livers pale and lustihood deject.
>
> (II.2.46–50)

His refusal to recognize reason makes it impossible for him to see things as they are, and leads him into inconsistency and confusion. What manhood and honour demand, and what reason would reject, is the recognition of Helen as a worthy pretext for the continuation of the war. She is, Troilus says,

> ... a pearl
> Whose price hath launched above a thousand ships,
> And turned crowned kings to merchants.
>
> (II.2.82–4)

This, however, puts him in the contradictory position of denying his opinion, expressed in the play's opening scene, that Helen is *not* an object worth fighting for:

> Fools on both sides! Helen must needs be fair,
> When with your blood you daily paint her thus.
> I cannot fight upon this argument;
> It is too starved a subject for my sword.
>
> (I.1.92–5)

His support for Helen is a wilful self-blinding; carried away once more by his own rhetoric, he is here more concerned with what he sees as honour than with truth. It is of the same kind that prevents him from seeing that Cressida is incapable of a 'winnowed purity in love'. In both cases the consequence of his idealism is disaster: the personal disaster of Cressida's devastating betrayal, and the communal disaster of the destruction of Troy brought about through a hot-headed continuation of a war that could have been brought to an end.

Clearly, Troilus' idealism and the feelings it generates in him need to be subjected to a careful scrutiny. At the outset of the play the love that he sees as ennobling has nevertheless taken away his will to fight:

> ... I am weaker than a woman's tear,
> Tamer than sleep, fonder than ignorance,
> Less valiant than the virgin in the night,
> And skilless as unpractised infancy.
>
> (I.1.9–12)

There is nothing self-critical in this confession of what he later calls 'womanish' feelings; Troilus presents himself in images of childhood, inexperience and femininity for the approval of Pandarus and, more crucially, for his own approval. Now it would be quite possible to argue that this effect of love is a civilizing one, turning the lover away from the brutalities of war, but this argument is hardly applicable in the case of Troilus who contradicts his own account of himself when, at the end of this very same scene, he goes off with Aeneas to rejoin the 'sport' of battle. We may note here that Troilus has a marked tendency to use a very self-conscious rhetoric. His statement that love has made him 'weaker than a woman's tear' produces four further comparisons in a matter of three lines, but they add nothing to the meaning expressed in the initial one. His language, here as elsewhere, is highly conventional and artificial and also highly self-absorbed, and has the effect of setting him at a distance from what he is saying. We might suspect that he is not describing how he feels so much as how he thinks he ought to feel, striking the pose of an unrequited lover. The same might be said of his description of Cressida, the cause of the 'cruel battle' in his heart, for he presents her too through rather strained and conventional comparisons: the white of her hand makes other whites seem like ink, and its softness makes the cygnet's down seem harsh; her chastity is akin to that of Daphne, who suffered metamorphosis into a laurel bush rather than succumbing to Apollo's advances; she is a pearl that can only be achieved by a perilous voyage (and we should note that this last is precisely the same image as the one he uses to try to define the worth of Helen in the Trojan debate). Shakespeare mocked this kind of comparison in Sonnet 130:

> My mistress' eyes are nothing like the sun;
> Coral is far more red than her lips red;
> If snow be white, why then her breasts are dun;
> If hairs be wires, black wires grow on her head.

Troilus' images do not describe Cressida in any way, for it becomes clear that he has never met her; the love that he claims to feel for her has no firm foundation, being based on no actual knowledge of her. His rather studied (and, as we see when we meet her, rather inappropriate) comparisons are the attributes of an idea of her that he has generated for himself.

Troilus, in effect, is creating himself in the refined image of a courtly lover and creating Cressida in the image of an object worthy of such a love. The juxtaposition of his flights of rhetorical verse with the matter-of-fact prose of Pandarus lays open to question the reality of these images, however, and his elevation of his passion is undermined by the much more mundane suggestiveness of Pandarus' comparison of his promotion of the relationship between Troilus and Cressida to baking a cake. The materialism of this analogy is echoed in the ambiguity of Troilus' own comparison of Cressida to a pearl, which on the one hand contains overtones of spirituality and purity (as in the biblical 'pearl of great price'), but on the other hand makes her into an object to be bought by a merchant-Troilus with the aid of Pandarus. And the harbour to which he hopes to be carried by 'this sailing Pandar' is, precisely, 'her bed'.

The impression of Troilus with which we are left at the end of the opening scene is of a collection of contradictions: he believes himself to be profoundly in love with a woman whom he has never met; he claims to be more long-suffering than the goddess Patience herself, yet is desperately impatient to 'come to' Cressida; he does not see the erotic motive of the passion he has for this 'stubborn-chaste' woman; he is at one moment debilitated by his love, at the next anxious to be off to fight. He is a very confused young man who nevertheless firmly believes that whatever he believes to be true *is* true, and it is this absolute belief in the rightness of his impressions that he takes into the Trojan debate. Here, we must be struck immediately by the irony of the fact that the Troilus who, when we last saw him, was very clearly aware of the true value of Helen, has now converted her into an ideal,

> . . . a theme of honour and renown,
> A spur to valiant and magnanimous deeds,
> Whose present courage may beat down our foes,
> And fame in time to come canonize us.
>
> (II.2.200–203)

What kind of constant man is this? There is, no doubt, something attractive about the single-minded vehemence of his arguments in this scene and about his insistence on setting honour above prudence, but we should not let that obscure the fact that those arguments are made in support of something he did not support a few scenes ago, and that they are unfair (as when he counters Helenus' indication of the irrationality of his position by implying that Helenus is a coward), spurious (as when he says that a thief is unworthy of the thing he has stolen if he is afraid to keep it), and illogical (not surprisingly, since he denies the authority of reason). And, worst of all, they are calamitous, for they throw away the last opportunity to save the city.

During this scene Troilus becomes involved in a discussion of the meaning of value that pervades the play, and associates himself firmly with a relativist position. 'What's aught but as 'tis valued?' (II.2.53) he asks, and goes on to suggest that the value of anything is given to it by an act of will on the part of the valuer:

> I take today a wife, and my election
> Is led on in the conduct of my will,
> My will enkindled by mine eyes and ears,
> Two traded pilots 'twixt the dangerous shores
> Of will and judgement: how may I avoid,
> Although my will distaste what it elected,
> The wife I chose?
>
> (II.2.62–8)

The emotive force makes this argument, at first sight, difficult to deny, but it relies upon a complex use of the word 'will' which to the Eliza-bethans had two essential meanings: not only volition or determination, but also sexual desire or lust. The opposition that Troilus sets up between will and judgement is therefore ironic and reflects a deep moral confusion when he characterizes judgement as 'dangerous'. This makes his choice of the example of a husband's duty to his wife all the more unfortunate; no doubt it is prompted by thoughts of Cressida, but it ignores the fact (later pointed out by Hector) that the wife who has been taken by the Trojans and who is the subject of the debate belongs to someone else. Furthermore, since Troilus argues that value is relative, it would seem contradictory for him to claim that a choice once made is irrevocable; it would appear more logical to argue that if value is given by an act of will, an act of will can also take it away.

Here, in effect, Troilus rejects reason and judgement while giving absolute value to the choices of his will, by which he appears to mean his particular feelings. This explains much of what happens to him in his relationship with Cressida. Having created an image of her, and having chosen to love that image, he cannot understand what is happening when the real Cressida fails to act in accordance with his image. The tensions are set up explicitly in his speech at the end of the assignation scene:

> O that I thought it could be in a woman –
> As, if it can, I will presume in you –
> To feed for aye her lamp and flames of love;
> To keep her constancy in plight and youth,
> Outliving beauty's outward, with a mind
> That doth renew swifter than blood decays!
> Or that persuasion could but thus convince me,
> That my integrity and truth to you
> Might be affronted with the match and weight
> Of such a winnowed purity in love –
> How were I then uplifted! But alas,
> I am as true as truth's simplicity,
> And simpler than the infancy of truth.
>
> (III.2.156–68)

Troilus' image of constancy would make near-impossible demands on any woman, and particularly on a woman whom he has only just met, though the vehemence of his presentation convinces Cressida for the moment that she is capable of the constancy that he requires. At the same time, we should note that there is a strong element of egotism here, with his repeated emphasis on the excellence of his own feelings ('my

integrity', 'How were I then uplifted', 'I am as true as truth's simplicity'),
which recurs in his final speech to Cressida (IV.4.101–7) when he again
insists on his 'truth'. This egotism is an aspect of the self-absorption
that characterizes all his dealings with Cressida:

> I am giddy; expectation whirls me round.
> Th' imaginary relish is so sweet
> That it enchants my sense. What will it be,
> When that the watery palate tastes indeed
> Love's thrice-repurèd nectar? – death, I fear me,
> Swooning destruction . . .
>
> (III.2.16–21)

As his appeal to appetite here implies, his feelings have very little to do
with the actual Cressida, and much to do with his rhetorical inflation of
his desires, both for higher truth and for sensual experience.

Because the Cressida he sees is the creation of his own will, it is all the
more difficult for Troilus to comprehend what is happening when he is
forced to look at the real thing. He watches her promise herself to
Diomedes with growing horror, and at first tries to deny the evidence of
his senses:

> But if I tell how these two did co-act,
> Shall I not lie in publishing a truth?
> Sith yet there is a credence in my heart,
> An esperance so obstinately strong,
> That doth invert th' attest of eyes and ears,
> As if those organs had deceptious functions,
> Created only to calumniate.
> Was Cressid here?
>
> (V.2.120–27)

What he has seen cannot be true because the Cressida he has idealized
could not behave in this way. What until this moment had seemed a
simple, single truth is now divided, bewildering Troilus, who cannot
reconcile Diomedes' Cressida with his own:

> O madness of discourse,
> That cause sets up with and against itself!
> Bifold authority, where reason can revolt
> Without perdition, and loss assume all reason
> Without revolt. This is, and is not, Cressid!
>
> (V.2.145–9)

The tormented rhetoric of this speech reflects Troilus' attempt to come
to terms with what he cannot understand, bringing him to a point where

the love that had tickled his palate disintegrates and is converted to something revolting to his appetite:

> The fractions of her faith, orts of her love,
> The fragments, scraps, the bits, and greasy relics
> Of her o'er-eaten faith, are bound to Diomed.
> (V.2.161–3)

He survives by converting his love for Cressida into a hatred of Diomedes, and for the remainder of the play is driven by a rage that cannot be restrained and is expressed in a new kind of rhetoric:

> And, thou great-sized coward,
> Nor space of earth shall sunder our two hates;
> I'll haunt thee like a wicked conscience still,
> That mouldeth goblins swift as frenzy's thoughts.
> (V.10.26–9)

This is very different from the idealism of his earlier manner, but in its unrealistic and violent bombast it is just as far from reason.

Troilus is, as Ulysses says, immature. His need to idealize his motivations, his belief in honour no less than his love, is in part a matter of youth and inexperience, and we can feel a degree of sympathy for him. But he is very much the creator of his own problems, and his insistence on a kind of ideal that is contrary to the dictates of reason can only lead to division and disintegration. Furthermore, his self-absorption and his ability to obscure his egotism in elevated rhetoric and thus romanticize the imperatives of his own will are not attractive. He is a hero, but he is a flawed and unsatisfactory one, and he leaves the play having derived no saving perception from his experience beyond the recognition that words (but he means only the words of others and fails to see the complicity of his own) may have no matter behind them.

Cressida and the Position of Women

Of the two young lovers, Cressida had received by far the crueller treatment at the hands of history when Shakespeare chose to tell her story, and she has received the crueller treatment at the hands of critics since then. The literary tradition as it was understood by the Elizabethans presented her as the embodiment not merely of infidelity, but of cold calculation, since she was thought to have played the whore even before her betrayal of Troilus; it is this tradition that Pistol in *Henry V* echoes when he refers to a 'lazar kite of Cressid's kind' (II.1.73), a kite being a bird of prey. There was not, of course, much that Shakespeare could do to put her infidelity into a softer light, since he was constrained by the shape of the story he took over, but some of the changes he did make had the effect of further darkening the moral tone of her character. For example, Chaucer's Criseyde is a widow, which explains her sexual knowingness; in a supposedly inexperienced young girl, such knowingness is less acceptable. The behaviour of Shakespeare's Cressida also seems worse because of the limitations imposed by the dramatic form: the necessary telescoping of incidents to fit the brief time available in a play makes her capitulation to Diomedes seem much quicker and more brutally heartless than that of Chaucer's Criseyde, who benefits from the extended treatment that Chaucer was able to give to it.

Cressida's emotions are, no doubt, shallow, and it is not difficult to give a reading of her character that makes her seem hard and calculating. She is not, certainly, the 'stubborn-chaste' woman Troilus imagines in the opening scene. She is excessively fond of bawdy talk and passionately interested in the empty goings-on at court. She has a manipulative intelligence that makes her more than a match for Pandarus, and that makes suspect her behaviour with Troilus. Her soliloquy at the end of I.2 that reveals her feelings for Troilus also reveals her determination to keep full control over the situation:

> Yet hold I off. Women are angels, wooing;
> Things won are done; joy's soul lies in the doing.
> That she beloved knows naught that knows not this:
> Men prize the thing ungained more than it is.
> That she was never yet that ever knew
> Love got so sweet as when desire did sue;
> Therefore this maxim out of love I teach:
> 'Achievement is command; ungained, beseech.'
> Then, though my heart's content firm love doth bear,
> Nothing of that shall from mine eyes appear.
>
> (I.2.286–95)

But when Pandarus brings the two young people together she does reveal her feelings, and we may wonder whether this is part of a game she is playing with Troilus, whether the fears and doubts she expresses are nothing more than a pretence of modesty:

> My lord, I do beseech you, pardon me;
> 'Twas not my purpose thus to beg a kiss.
> I am ashamed – O heavens, what have I done?
> For this time will I take my leave, my lord.
>
> (III.2.134–7)

59

She wins him by pretending a kind of innocence that fits well with his ideal image of her, but is hard to credit in view of the bawdy talk that passes between her and Pandarus. In the morning, when Troilus is ready to leave her, she fears that she may have miscalculated, that her game of hard-to-get has not gone on long enough. From her claim that 'You men will never tarry' (IV.2.16) one might infer a knowledge of sexual affairs unfitting for the innocent girl that she has presented to Troilus, and she shows neither modesty nor shame, nor even embarrassment, when her uncle returns with his leering, voyeuristic interest in what the lovers have been doing. Her exasperation here is clearly not to be taken seriously:

> Go hang yourself, you naughty mocking uncle!
> You bring me to do – and then you flout me too.
>
> (IV.2.25–6)

And her banter with Troilus is now of an openly sexual nature that she would certainly have suppressed in her pre-coital state:

> My lord, come you again into my chamber;
> You smile and mock me, as if I meant naughtily.
>
> (IV.2.36–7)

It would be difficult not to see this Cressida as a wanton, and her forwardness with the Greek leaders, when she allows herself to be kissed by all of them, seems to clinch the matter, justifying Ulysses' characterization of her:

> There's a language in her eye, her cheek, her lip,
> Nay, her foot speaks; her wanton spirits look out
> At every joint and motive of her body.
> O, these encounterers, so glib of tongue,
> That give accosting welcome ere it comes,
> And wide unclasp the tables of their thoughts
> To every tickling reader! Set them down
> For sluttish spoils of opportunity
> And daughters of the game.
>
> (IV.5.55–63)

We are not surprised that Diomedes has already become her 'sweet guardian' by the evening of the very day on which she left Troilus; he has clearly much more experience of such women than Troilus, and his rough off-handedness gives him control over her, so that Troilus is forced to watch his 'stubborn-chaste' mistress pursuing the 'unworthy' Greek. Her misgivings about giving Troilus' sleeve to Diomedes seem at best perfunctory. She has condemned herself to being the false Cressid of history no more than twenty-four hours after swearing eternal love to Troilus.

And yet this is not all that we can say about Cressida. She is not, it is true, the high-soaring goddess that Troilus thinks her, but it is reasonable to ask how far she can be blamed for not being the woman Troilus wants (and therefore imagines) her to be. Her early determination not to reveal her feelings to Troilus could be seen as something other than calculation, as a healthy awareness of the dangers involved in her position. After all, Troilus is not offering her marriage or any other kind of honest, open relationship; all he is offering to do is set her up as his mistress in a clandestine affair that seems ironic in view of his insistence that his is a strained pure love. There seems no reason to believe that her feelings for Troilus are not real, or that her fears about his constancy are part of a performance. When, before the two of them go off to bed, Troilus builds up his hyperbolical vision of eternal love, she competes with his vows because she is carried away by his rhetoric and is persuaded to believe that she really is capable of such fidelity. And perhaps, if circumstances had been different, she would have been.

Cressida does not, after all, have very much reason to trust anyone. Betrayal is a way of life in her family. Her father betrayed his country and left her behind in the care of her uncle. Pandarus betrays her by acting as pandar to Troilus, just as her father will later betray her again by acting as pandar to Diomedes. When Aeneas brings the news that Cressida must go to Troy, Troilus' first thought is to tell Aeneas to keep secret the fact that he is at Cressida's house, while Cressida reacts with a passionate refusal to go:

> Tear my bright hair, and scratch my praised cheeks;
> Crack my clear voice with sobs, and break my heart
> With sounding 'Troilus'. I will not go from Troy.
>
> (IV.2.106–8)

This can hardly be calculation, since there would be no reason for it at this point. The feeling, however superficial, must certainly be real. Again, when she allows herself to be kissed by the Greek leaders, we might ask ourselves what choice she has. She is not, after all, in a position of much power here, and it is noteworthy that she does not speak until after she has been kissed by Agamemnon, Nestor, Achilles and Patroclus, as if she were not able to summon enough presence of mind until then. Nestor is impressed by the way she handles this situation, and calls her a 'woman of quick sense'; it is in reply to this that Ulysses produces his crushing characterization of her, but it should also be noted that it is Ulysses' idea that she should be kissed in general, as if he wished to humiliate her. He creates a Cressida, just as Troilus created another, but perhaps neither of them is the definitive one. And perhaps we can understand why, finding herself vulnerable and without a protector – 'A woeful Cressid 'mongst the merry Greeks' (I V.4.55) – she should be so anxious to find herself a 'Sweet guardian' in Diomedes.

Cressida's situation illustrates the limitations under which women lived in Shakespeare's England (and in a play that is very much concerned with those limitations, a certain poignancy must have been generated by the fact that women's roles on the stage were played by boys). Although the monarch was a queen, she ruled over a profoundly patriarchal society. Marriages were not contracted for romantic but for economic and political reasons, and a daughter, therefore, was very much a form of currency; she could not give her body in marriage, but was given in marriage by her father. She thus became an object to be possessed: both Cressida and Helen are described as pearls, Antenor is used to 'buy' Cressida (I I I.3.28), and Paris responds to Diomedes' view of Helen in similar mercantile terms:

> Fair Diomed, you do as chapmen do,
> Dispraise the thing that you desire to buy;
> But we in silence hold this virtue well:
> We'll not commend what we intend to sell.
>
> (I V.1.76–9)

By giving herself Cressida has transgressed, has broken the patriarchal rule, and is devalued into a whore. Helen too is a whore in these terms, as Thersites points out: 'All the argument is a whore and a cuckold' (II.3.71–2), but she, presumably, can be revalued, made legitimate again, by returning to her marriage. This is why the question of her value is at the centre of the Trojan debate, while it never arises at all in the Greek debate.

In giving her body Cressida has acted in a manner that is a man's prerogative, as she herself is aware:

> But though I loved you well, I wooed you not;
> And yet, good faith, I wished myself a man,
> Or that we women had men's privilege
> Of speaking first.
>
> (III.2.124–7)

The socially destructive result of the pursuit of relationships generated by erotic desire outside marriage is seen in the debilitating effect that it has on the men who become involved in (or perhaps, in this play, victimized by) them. Troilus, Paris and Achilles are all disarmed by women, putting desire before duty, either social or personal. Troilus and Paris are kept from the battle by their women, and Achilles even makes himself a traitor for Polyxena:

> Fall Greeks; fail fame; honour or go or stay;
> My major vow lies here; this I'll obey.
> (V.1.40–41)

The 'fallen' women of the play, therefore, are shown to have only negative authority, and yet there seems to be no possibility of positive authority or influence even for a woman in a more legitimate position. Cassandra is a prophetess and always speaks truth, but her intrusion into the Trojan debate is simply dismissed by Troilus as madness, and she has no effect on Hector when she predicts his death and the doom of Troy.

Of more significance is the role of Andromache, who has a function within a larger debate on marriage. In his speech on degree, Ulysses says that the effect of disorder is to disrupt the 'unity and married calm of states' (I.3.100), linking the idea of marriage with peace and unity on a political level. In the Trojan debate, Troilus and Hector use the idea of marriage to support opposing attitudes to the value of Helen, Troilus claiming that a choice of a wife is irrevocable, while Hector, taking a position that Ulysses would applaud, points out that the logical conclusion of this unarguable view is that Helen should be returned to her husband, something that both natural and political laws demand, since there is no 'nearer debt in all humanity/Than wife is to the husband' (II.2.176–7). In his challenge to the Greeks, Hector raises his own wife to a principle worth fighting for, since she is 'wiser, fairer, truer' than any Greek lady (including Helen, who is the principle for which they are all fighting). We might expect, therefore, that this figure of courtesy would offer in his own relationship a model to set against the illegitimate ones. Yet in this marriage Andromache clearly does not have the authority that her wisdom and truth would seem to merit. The first thing we hear of her is that she has been scolded by Hector because of his shame at being defeated by Ajax, and on the only occasion on which she appears she is angrily dismissed by Hector for trying to persuade him not to fight. We are offered no relationship between man and woman better than this.

The play does not in any way attempt to condone Cressida's behaviour, although it is worth remembering once again the point that worried Dryden: that she goes unpunished for her infidelity. Her punishment, of course, exists in the future, outside the play but acknowledged by it, when Cressida will be punished eternally by her reputation:

> ... yet let memory,
> From false to false, among false maids in love,
> Upbraid my falsehood!
>
> (III.2.187–9)

She gives herself to Troilus out of social and moral weakness, and she betrays him for the same reasons. And yet her actions are not entirely a matter of moral laxity, for she is also a victim, made vulnerable because she is betrayed by masculine authority invested in her father and uncle, and judged (by masculine authority) and condemned because she acts in a situation where only passivity is expected of women. In this she can be taken to be representative of all women in such a society, married or unmarried, and because of this we can have sympathy for her.

Hector: Heroism and Tragedy

If any character in the play comes close to the heroic it is Hector, and indeed for the Elizabethans it was he rather than Achilles who was the hero of the *Iliad*. He was the embodiment of courtesy and valour, of what in the Middle Ages had become the principles of chivalry. Shakespeare allows his own Hector to keep these virtues, making him an idealist who believes that a warrior can conduct himself like a gentleman, and giving him a sense of what is valuable, a moral intelligence that is shared by no one in the play except, perhaps, Ulysses. He is admired by everyone with whom he has dealings, friend and enemy alike, with the single exception of Achilles. He endeavours to conduct his life along the lines laid down by his principle of 'fair play', and it is this, what Troilus calls his 'vice of mercy', that makes him terminate his combat with Ajax as well as his first encounter with Achilles. It is the opposite of the pitiless attitude that Troilus promotes and Achilles embodies, and it is obviously morally superior; and yet, as his death demonstrates, it is inadequate in the context of the war in which he is involved.

Hector's prime duty is to protect Troy, and the position he takes in the Trojan debate would achieve this: conciliation with the Greeks and an immediate end to bloodshed are available if the Trojans give up Helen. In the course of the debate he withdraws from this position, however, so that he is left only with the alternative of military defence of Troy. He is, as Ulysses points out, the 'base and pillar' of the city, and its safety, which it is his public duty to ensure, depends entirely upon his own. Hector also has a sense of private value which he defines as 'honour', and which drives him to set his own interest above the public good. He is a deeply divided figure, and finally as liable as any other character to be deflected from his own right understanding by personal desire. This ambivalence is prepared for even before he appears on stage, when Alexander describes his pique at being defeated in combat by Ajax:

> Hector, whose patience
> Is as a virtue fixed, today was moved:
> He chid Andromache, and struck his armourer ...
>
> (I.2.4–6)

His reaction to defeat, to a blemish on his honour, is surely a form of pride; it makes us question the strength of the patience for which he is celebrated, and it also moves him to acts that are hardly consonant with his reputation for courtesy.

It is this same flaw of pride, presumably, that accounts for his *volte face* in the debate. His arguments against keeping Helen rest on a realistic understanding of her value and of the futility of wasting more lives in her defence, and he easily demonstrates the irrationality and excessive passion on which his brothers' arguments are founded:

> The reasons you allege do more conduce
> To the hot passion of distempered blood
> Than to make up a free determination
> 'Twixt right and wrong; for pleasure and revenge
> Have ears more deaf than adders to the voice
> Of any true decision.
>
> (II.2.169–74)

The firm commitment here indicated to reason, right and truth is not easy to reconcile with Hector's capitulation to his brothers. He reverses his position because, he says, keeping Helen is a matter that affects their 'joint and several dignities' – that is, their reputation and honour, which too is a matter of pride. He appears, in fact, to have had no real wish to return Helen, but to have been playing a game with his brothers, for if he had had any intention of putting an end to the war he would hardly have sent Aeneas with his challenge to the Greeks, which he had already done before the debate began.

Hector is no more immune to confusion than anyone else. There is something attractive about the style of his challenge to the Greeks:

> Hector, in view of Trojans and of Greeks,
> Shall make it good, or do his best to do it,
> He hath a lady, wiser, fairer, truer,
> Than ever Greek did compass in his arms ...
> (I.3.273–6)

It is the challenge of a medieval knight offering single combat in the name of his lady, and attractive though it may be, it is quite preposterous in the brutal context of this war. It is, of course, what we might expect of a man who sees heroism in terms of chivalry, and who to some degree sees the war as a game (the Trojans in general share this attitude: at the end of the opening scene Troilus and Aeneas go off to the 'good sport' of the fight, and there is often something playful in Aeneas' treatment of his enemies, as with the light-hearted insolence of his manner in delivering the challenge, or the good humour of his banter with Diomedes), but it is at odds with the realism of his assessment of Helen, and reflects a self-delusion about the nature of war that is in some ways parallel to Troilus' illusions about love.

The climax of Hector's confusion comes in the scene in which he prepares for his final battle. Against the persuasions of his wife, who has dreamed of turbulence and slaughter, he insists on going out to fight. He further refuses to listen either to the prophecy of Cassandra or to the prohibition of his father. 'You know me dutiful,' he says to his father, while insisting on being released from that duty. The reason for his insistence is that he is engaged to fight many Greeks; the irony of this is that we have already seen Achilles change his mind about fighting because of his own prior vow to Polyxena. Achilles, that is, puts the wishes of Polyxena above his personal honour, while Hector puts *his* personal honour above the wishes of his wife and the safety of Troy:

> Mine honour keeps the weather of my fate.
> Life every man holds dear, but the dear man
> Holds honour far more precious-dear than life.
> (V.3.26–8)

This scene presents the culmination of a series of images that, taken together, indicate that Hector's concept of honour does reflect a confusion of values. His angry dismissal of Andromache echoes Alexander's account of his treatment of her after his defeat at the hands of Ajax. His refusal to respect her wishes sits uncomfortably with his challenge to the Greeks, in which he claims to be fighting for his lady, as well as with his argument about marriage in the debate: 'What nearer debt in all humanity/Than wife is to the husband?' (II.2.176–7). He has lost sight of the greater good in his eagerness for the satisfaction of his personal honour, which is itself an illusion, as Cassandra's final words clearly indicate: 'Thou dost thyself and all our Troy deceive' (V.3.90).

Hector's death is terrible, and painful for the audience, but its circumstances deprive it of any tragic feeling. His courtesy to Achilles at their first meeting, when the Greek is too tired to fight, makes all the more contemptible the manner in which Achilles kills him, which is in effect gang-murder. But the death is anti-climactic and deprived of any dignity, and the lurid rhetoric of Achilles' final speech turns it into melodrama:

> The dragon wing of night o'erspreads the earth,
> And, stickler-like, the armies separates.
> My half-supped sword, that frankly would have fed,
> Pleased with his dainty bait, thus goes to bed.
> Come, tie his body to the horse's tail;
> Along the field I will the Trojan trail.
>
> (V.8.17–22)

The force to which Hector falls victim is at once less rational and less moral than he is. And perhaps he fails to be a tragic hero because, however well-meaning he may be, he is finally playing the wrong game by the wrong rules. Certainly his view of the way a war should be conducted is ethically superior to the savage opportunism of Achilles, as it is to the foolhardy violence of Troilus, his courtesy preferable to the cynical realism of his enemies. But in the end, if a war is to be fought, what matters is victory. When the Trojans debate whether or not to return Helen to the Greeks, Hector articulates the rational response to the situation and then rejects it. In doing so he leaves himself prey to irrational forces that his own generosity of spirit cannot comprehend. 'Fie, savage, fie!' he says when Troilus advises him to be pitiless to his enemies, and he is right. But he is also wrong, and it is the fact that he cannot see how he is wrong that deprives his death of tragic significance. He is physically unarmed when Achilles kills him, but it is his lack of understanding of the realities of the war that actually unarms him and makes his death a lesser thing than it might have been.

Ulysses: Order, Rhetoric and Policy

In the Homeric tradition Ulysses, known to the Greeks as Odysseus, was admirable because of the resourcefulness and versatility of his intelligence (he it was who thought up the ruse of the wooden horse, thus bringing an end to the Trojan War), and therefore worthy of being made the hero of an epic poem. There was a post-Homeric tradition that was suspicious of such intelligence, however, equating it with deceitfulness and cunning, and because Odysseus' cleverness was closely associated with rhetoric, the persuasive use of language, this too was suspect. In *Troilus and Cressida* Ulysses is a master of rhetoric; like Hector, he wishes to act in accordance with intelligence and the moral sense, and he is, supremely, associated with the desire for order. There is, consequently, an inevitable tendency to assume that the position he articulates is close to Shakespeare's own, especially because his great speech on degree embodies the official Tudor doctrine that has become known as 'the Elizabethan world picture'. At the same time, we must be aware of a counter-impulse in the play, a recognition of the ways in which rhetoric can be used to manipulate.

According to Elizabethan doctrine, the entire universe is organized as a series of hierarchies which replicate one another. The hierarchy that forms the pattern for all others is that which has God as its head and descends through levels of angels, men, animals and birds, and the vegetable and mineral worlds; it is sometimes called the 'Great Chain of Being'. Within the various levels of the hierarchy there are others that emulate it: the sun is the head of the hierarchy of heavenly bodies, the lion of animals, the eagle of birds, gold of minerals. The human body is a hierarchy, and so are its abstract functions: reason must be in control. Social order rightly follows the same pattern. The major system has the king at its head (much royal symbolism derives from the Great Chain of being, which is why royal emblems tend to incorporate the sun, or the lion, or the rose), and minor systems are organized in the same way, with fathers over children, older brothers over younger, husbands over wives, and so on. Social order is validated by the fact that it is an image of cosmic order, the microcosm (man and his creation) replicating the macrocosm (the creation of God). This is the basis of Ulysses' speech:

> The heavens themselves, the planets, and this centre
> Observe degree, priority, and place,
> Insisture, course, proportion, season, form,
> Office, and custom, in all line of order.
> And therefore is the glorious planet Sol
> In noble eminence enthroned and sphered
> Amidst the other; whose med'cinable eye
> Corrects the ill aspects of planets evil,
> And posts like the commandment of a king,
> Sans check, to good and bad.
>
> (I.3.85–94)

The ideas in this speech were commonplace in Shakespeare's time, and were hardly original even before then; sources and analogues have been found in Homer, Virgil, Ovid, Chaucer, Elyot, Hooker, and other more obscure writers, but what is important is the fact that they were commonplace precisely because they were official Tudor doctrine. The significance that Ulysses' speech would have had for an Elizabethan audience can be gauged if we compare it with the Homily on obedience first published in 1547, and regularly read in churches:

Almighty God hath created and appointed all things in heaven, earth and waters, in a most excellent and perfect order. In heaven, he hath appointed distinct and several orders and states of Archangels and Angels. In earth he hath assigned and appointed Kings, Princes, with other governors under them, in all good and necessary order. The water above is kept, and raineth down in due time and season, The Sun, Moon, Stars, Rainbow, Thunder, Lightning, Clouds, and all Birds of the air, do keep their order. The Earth, Trees, seeds, plants, herbs, corn, grass, and all manner of beasts, keep themselves in order, all the parts of the year, as Winter, Summer, Months, nights and days, continue in their order . . .

Ulysses makes the same appeal to heavenly harmony as the master-pattern for all things.

The real force of the Homily does not lie in the fact that it expresses a noble conception of universal order, however; what is more important is that it provides a powerful instrument for the imposition of law and social order:

. . . every degree of people in their vocation, calling and office, hath appointed to them their duty and order: some are in high degree, some in low, some Kings and Princes, some inferiors and subjects, Priests, and lay-men, Masters and Servants, Fathers and Children, Husbands and Wives, rich and poor . . .

It is, in effect, a doctrine that validates the status quo: the way things are is the way they should be; whatever is, is good. The most important part of Ulysses' account of the overturning of degree is not his vision of cosmic chaos, but the possibility of social revolution that it implies:

How could communities,
Degrees in schools, and brotherhoods in cities,
Peaceful commerce from dividable shores,
The primogenitive and due of birth,
Prerogative of age, crowns, sceptres, laurels,
But by degree, stand in authentic place?
Take but degree away, untune that string,
And hark what discord follows! Each thing meets
In mere oppugnancy: the bounded waters

> Should lift their bosoms higher than the shores,
> And make a sop of all this solid globe;
> Strength should be lord of imbecility,
> And the rude son should strike his father dead;
> Force should be right, or, rather, right and wrong –
> Between whose endless jar justice resides –
> Should lose their names, and so should justice too.
>
> (I.3.103–18)

It is no wonder that Ulysses has so frequently been seen as the representative of Shakespeare's own attitude, with the official Elizabethan policy standing behind it.

Like everything else in this play, however, the position of Ulysses has its ambiguities. The universal hierarchical order is a noble concept, but it can be used to legitimize an unjust or ineffectual rule, and Ulysses is quite clearly using the concept for political ends: to restore authority to Agamemnon. Yet it is in large part the fault of Agamemnon that the Greek army is in disorder, for, as Ulysses points out, 'The specialty of rule hath been neglected' (I.3.78), and it seems that the general has abandoned any claim to authority by putting responsibility for the failure of the Greeks into the hands of the gods. Ulysses relates reason and order, finding the major symptom of the disease of irrationality or disorder in the insubordination of Achilles, the pride that has prompted his withdrawal from combat. But having identified this central cause of the Greek failure, Ulysses does not seem to know how to remedy it. Faced with the political reality of the intransigent Achilles, reason offers no ready answers, and the best that Ulysses can come up with is the opportunistic ruse, prompted by the challenge brought by Aeneas, of deflating Achilles by inflating Ajax. The spokesman for hierarchy is forced to promote the lesser man over the greater, and the result of his endeavour is an increase in disorder when Ajax is as badly infected by pride as Achilles.

There is, we must acknowledge, a gap between the elevated vision that Ulysses proposes and the practical reality of the situation he wishes to remedy, with the result that he uses his rhetoric for its persuasive power, for its style rather than its content, and for all his high ideals he is not above bending the truth in order to achieve his ends. This is most apparent in his conversation with Achilles about time and reputation. We may be carried away, as Achilles is, by the eloquence of this account of the effects of 'envious and calumniating time', but we must note that it depends on the misrepresentation by Ulysses of his own beliefs, and on a claim about the Greeks' attitude to Ajax that he knows is untrue. He says

That no man is the lord of any thing,
Though in and of him there is much consisting,
Till he communicate his parts to others;
Nor doth he of himself know them for aught
Till he behold them formèd in th' applause
Where they're extended . . .

(III.3.115–20)

A man's merits exist only as they are valued by others; in its ethical relativism the view Ulysses here expresses is close to that of Troilus: 'What's aught but as 'tis valued?' (II.2.53), and very far from the belief in absolute values inherent in the concept of degree. Furthermore, the claim that 'all the Greeks begin to worship Ajax' (III.3.182) is simply not true. It is a continuation of the piece of theatre in which the Greek leaders pretend to ignore Achilles, a cunning, possibly cynical attempt at manipulation.

Because Ulysses *sounds* authoritative it is easy to assign him the status of authority in the play and to give too much credence to his judgements. This is particularly true of the confident way in which he makes what appear to be definitive statements about character. We have already noted the discrepancy between his impression of Diomedes and our own. His description of Troilus (IV.5.96–112), presented with assurance, is something of an idealization of the young man (and probably close to the way Troilus would like to see himself), but turns out to be hearsay, got from Aeneas who would have good reason to present such a powerful picture to an enemy. More damaging is his characterization of Cressida (IV.5.55–63), since it has been so frequently echoed in critical history. There is nothing in the scene to justify his view of her; she is kissed in general because he suggests it, creating another of his little dramas. Her silence when she is first accosted suggests that she is taken aback by this treatment, while his contemptuous refusal to kiss her himself (note also his bitter references to Helen) indicates the misogyny that may underlie his attitude and that may make his reading of the 'language in her eye' a misreading.

Ulysses is the closest we can find in the play to a norm, but he is trapped by circumstances: he would like to live by reason and order, but he is forced by political reality to use trickery. He is also, perhaps, as prone as anyone else to fall victim to his own self-delusion, to believe that his judgements are infallible, which is why he miscalculates in his attempts to manipulate Achilles and Ajax. The irony of his position becomes clear if we note certain unflattering parallels that are brought out in the structure of the play. First, his attempts to exert power through language relate him to Thersites, as does his frequent use of theatre, which relates him also to Patroclus, whom he despises for his performances. Worse, his position in the war-plot as go-between for the Greek leaders and Achilles links his function to that of Pandarus. These parallels inevitably undercut his claim to dignity, and draw him into the circle of ambiguity that all the other characters inhabit.

Achilles: Pride and Desire

Unrivalled in martial prowess, Achilles is the hero of the *Iliad*, though his is a brutal kind of heroism: he is courageous and good at killing because he is bigger and stronger than anyone else. Shakespeare dismantles the Homeric view of heroism by giving his Achilles few positive qualities apart from his strength. If we judge by the adjectives most frequently used to describe him, other characters think of him mainly in terms of his size: he is 'great', 'large', 'broad'. The first account of him in the play, that of Ulysses, sees his value in terms of his strength as

> The great Achilles, whom opinion crowns
> The sinew and the forehand of our host . . .
> (I.3.142–3)

but we should note that this subtly undermines the reputation of Achilles by presenting it as a matter of opinion (that is, of image) rather than fact. Now we have to be careful about how we judge Ulysses' account of the behaviour of Achilles, because he is using it as part of a larger programme of persuasion; he sees Achilles as the infectious source of disorder in the Greek camp, and his highly dramatic recreation of the mockery of the leaders by Patroclus that Achilles is encouraging is intended to move them against Achilles. What most infuriates Ulysses about the behaviour of Achilles and Patroclus is its elevation of brawn and its concomitant denial of reason:

> They call this bed-work, mappery, closet-war;
> So that the ram that batters down the wall,
> For the great swing and rudeness of his poise,
> They place before his hand that made the engine,
> Or those that with the fineness of their souls
> By reason guide his execution.
> (I.3.205–10)

The contempt for reason for which Ulysses criticizes Achilles foreshadows Troilus' rejection of reason, relating the two men as victims of unruly will or irrational desire.

72

Achilles' irrationality is underlined by the fact that the play provides no motivation for his withdrawal from combat. In the *Iliad* Achilles had a genuine grievance: Agamemnon had used his prerogative as general to take from Achilles the girl Briseis who had been awarded to him as the spoils of war. Shakespeare gives him no such grievance, and when the Greek leaders try to speak with him he treats them with contempt, refusing to give any explanation of his behaviour. He seems to us as he seems to them: proud, arrogant, slothful, childish, and not very intelligent. If Thersites is lost in the labyrinth of his own fury, Achilles is lost in the labyrinth of his own pride, interested only in his image of himself,

> And never suffers matter of the world
> Enter his thoughts, save such as do revolve
> And ruminate himself . . .
>
> (II.3.184–6)

The disease that has caused such disorder within Achilles has also caused disorder within the Greek system, for his excessive pride in himself has caused disdain for his general, has offered to others a bad example for emulation, and has initiated the widespread 'neglection of degree'. A devastating commentary on this pride is provided through his most egregious emulator, the mongrel beef-witted lord Ajax, who has developed a pride as great as that of Achilles. He too has withdrawn to his tent, where he mocks the endeavours of the Greek leadership and encourages Thersites to perform even grosser pageants than those with which Patroclus entertains Achilles. Before his combat with Hector, his pride has so engulfed him, so filled him with delusions, that Thersites is able to hold him up as a mirror for Achilles' own mindless and monstrous arrogance:

> The man's undone for ever, for if Hector break not his neck i' th' combat, he'll break't himself in vainglory. He knows not me: I said 'Good morrow, Ajax' and he replies 'Thanks, Agamemnon.' – What think you of this man, that takes me for the general? He's grown a very land-fish, languageless, a monster. A plague of opinion!
>
> (III.3.257–64)

The point is that Ajax *is* a mirror-image of Achilles – not just a parody, but a replica, faithfully reflecting Achilles' disease back to him.

There is a further disturbance in Achilles which has to do with his relationship with Patroclus. When in V.1 Thersites calls Patroclus Achilles' 'masculine whore' and lays his usual curse of diseases on 'such preposterous discoveries' ('preposterous' meaning something that inverts

the order of nature), he is making the only explicit reference to homosexuality in Shakespeare's works. It is possible to argue, as some critics
have, that this is nothing more than the accusation of an envious slan-
derer, and that the words of affection that pass between Achilles and
Patroclus are nothing more than the conventional language of close
friendship between men, but Patroclus' lines to Achilles after Ulysses'
account of the effects of time on reputation seem to imply something
more than this:

> To this effect, Achilles, have I moved you.
> A woman impudent and mannish grown
> Is not more loathed than an effeminate man
> In time of action. I stand condemned for this;
> They think my little stomach to the war,
> And your great love to me, restrains you thus.
> Sweet, rouse yourself, and the weak wanton Cupid
> Shall from your neck unloose his amorous fold . . .
>
> (III.3.216–23)

It is difficult to ignore the strong suggestions of physical love here,
and it is hard to see how the implication of homosexuality can be
avoided. The Elizabethans did not, of course, have the same sexual
stereotypes that exist today, and their strong interest in transvestism
and androgyny indicates a much less clear-cut view of sexual roles
(Patroclus' references here to mannish women and effeminate men may
remind us of the frequency with which women disguise themselves as
men in Shakespearean comedy, and of the fact that female stage roles
were played by boys). Nevertheless, homosexuality was officially pro-
hibited, being a felony that could be punished by death. It was feared
and loathed because it was linked with other forms of disturbance: for
example, when Christopher Marlowe was accused of treason and atheism
he was also accused of sodomy. Homosexuality stood outside the world
of creation; according to the Elizabethan theologian Richard Hooker it
was not a part of nature, having no place in the Chain of Being. It is easy
to see why it should make an appearance in this particular play.

We may see in Achilles an emblem of psychic disturbance. Pride and
misdirected desire make him withdraw from combat and pass his time
with Patroclus on a lazy bed, and after Ulysses has shown him how his
wantonness has damaged his reputation, and has begun to motivate him
back into combat, Achilles' effeminacy is curiously re-directed and translated into a desire to see Hector:

> I have a woman's longing,
> An appetite that I am sick withal,
> To see great Hector in his weeds of peace . . .
> (III.3. 237–9)

He is once again disarmed by the amorous fold of weak wanton Cupid, however, when he receives the letter from Hecuba reminding him of his promise to Polyxena. Apparently unconcerned that to keep a vow made to a woman of the enemy will make him a traitor, he once again withdraws:

> Fall Greeks; fail frame; honour or go or stay;
> My major vow lies here; this I'll obey.
> (V.1.40–41)

At no point does Achilles act because of the requirements of the situation. Instead he is driven by his appetites, by desire. When he is finally provoked by the death of Patroclus to seek out Hector we may feel some sympathy for the human grief at great loss that moves him, but unfortunately it does not move him to noble action, but instead to the plotting and execution of gang-murder. His last act in the play is also his final abandonment of his heroic status, for he discredits the one virtue we have been able to find in him: the courage guaranteed by his strength.

Comedy and Satire: Pandarus and Thersites

Very different though they are, Pandarus and Thersites have similar functions in the two plots; each is involved in the action but each is also, in a sense, detached from it and thus able to provide a commentary on it. Within the love-plot Pandarus has a coarse but practical attitude to Troilus' courtship of Cressida, bringing down to earth the young man's romantic pretensions; because the effect he creates is unconscious it is essentially without malice, and the perspective he opens up on the self-delusion of Troilus and Cressida is a comic one. Within the war-plot Thersites provides a much more savage commentary on the motives of the Greek leaders, a savagery which in the last act is applied also to the motives of the lovers. The effects that he achieves are by no means unconscious, and his insistence on finding the dark, debased side of everything makes the tone of his commentary satiric rather than comic.

The Pandarus that Shakespeare found in Chaucer's *Troilus and Criseyde* is a young man, unsuccessful in love himself, and anxious to employ all his substantial energies to bring success to the affairs of his friend Troilus; although culpable, he is not unattractive. By making his Pandarus an old man, Shakespeare makes him so much the more unpleasant.

As Cressida's uncle he should act as her protector, but he makes himself the instrument of her betrayal. His bawdy humour is always slightly excessive, his sniggering involvement in the activities of the lovers a kind of voyeurism. His interests lie firmly in the trivial, in gossip and the fashionable doings at Helen's court. Even the war is of remote concern to him, important only when it aids or interferes with his projects. He uses the return from combat of the Trojan warriors (I.2) as a means of building up Troilus: by praising the valour of each hero and then insisting on Troilus' superiority, he hopes to make him attractive to Cressida. But the most telling thing about this episode is his contemptuous and snobbish dismissal of the common soldiers, who are, after all, willing to lay down their lives for the protection of people like Pandarus: 'Asses, fools, dolts; chaff and bran, chaff and bran; porridge after meat!' (I.2.241–2). He appears incapable of comprehending that anything in the world might be of more than material value.

It is this moral stupidity that deprives his activities of malice and makes them comic rather than satiric (although in this play even the comedy is harsh and the distinction is not always sharp). Although he is a fool he is well-meaning, and believes that he is doing good for Troilus and Cressida because he has no higher vision of love than the purely carnal, and this inevitably infects the affair he is promoting. Because of Troilus' association with and dependence on this base figure, his own motives are brought into question. The elevated romantic attitude presented in his verse is persistently undermined through its juxtaposition with Pandarus' colloquial prose, and we are made aware of the possibility of self-delusion in his vision of love by the pervasive materialism of Pandarus' treatment of the affair. Similarly, although Cressida demonstrates herself to be more intelligent than Pandarus, and well able to control him, his interest in bawdry and in the trivial activities of court life encourages the coarser and more superficial aspects of Cressida's character.

Pandarus achieves his most devastating effect in the scene in which he brings Troilus and Cressida together (III.2). His interference here at the moment when he is least needed, his insistence on treating them as if they were actors in a play he is directing, makes it difficult to believe in the sincerity of the lovers. The uncompromising crudity of his dialogue indicates the carnal reality of the meeting:

Alas the day, how loath you are to offend daylight! An 'twere dark, you'd close sooner. So, so, rub on, and kiss the mistress. How now, a kiss in fee-farm! Build there, carpenter, the air is sweet. – Nay, you shall fight your hearts out ere I part you: the falcon as the tercel, for all the ducks i' th' river – go to, go to.

(III.2.46–52)

The overt references to physicality here and to the violence of sexual union are sufficiently strong that they apparently disconcert the lovers themselves, for at the moment that should be the poetic climax of their love they speak in prose, as if infected by the carnal implications and unable to rise above them. The same effect is produced on the morning after their union, when this naughty mocking uncle destroys any possibilities of lyric grace in their awakening by his curiosity about the intimate details of their night. It becomes difficult even to take seriously the lovers' grief at parting, accompanied as it is by Pandarus' comic sentimentality, and his ability to comprehend feelings only through a perspective provided by the inanities of popular song:

What a pair of spectacles is here! Let me embrace too. 'O heart,' as the goodly saying is –

> '– O heart, heavy heart,
> Why sigh'st thou without breaking?'
> where he answers again:
> 'Because thou canst not ease thy smart
> By friendship nor by speaking.'

There was never a truer rhymae. Let us cast away nothing, for we may live to have need of such a verse. We see it, we see it, – How now, lambs!

(IV.4.13–22)

After this, which is really little more than noise, we are bound to smile at Troilus' grandiose claims to a love of such strained purity that it is envied by the gods. Pandarus serves, however unwittingly, to provide a critical perspective on the lovers, and especially on Troilus, by revealing the suppressed carnal element in this idealized love. This does not, of course, deny absolutely the possibility that the love is genuine, but serves to indicate the measure of self-delusion that it contains.

Pandarus is foolish but well-intentioned; Thersites is neither. The *Iliad* presented him as the most unpleasant of the Greeks at the Trojan conflict, an ugly and ill-natured jeerer, and he subsequently had a long literary career as the embodiment of malice. Shakespeare took this figure and added to it elements of the licensed fool, as is indicated by Achilles: 'He is a privileged man' (II.3.56). The stage fool derived from the traditional court fool who, because his words were taken as the expression of childishness or genuine folly (madness), had a protected position that allowed him to say whatever he wished, even to the king. Fools appear frequently on the Shakespearean stage (most notably in *Twelfth Night* and *King Lear*); as a theatrical device the fool was very useful, because he was able to articulate views that could not otherwise be expressed. Shakespeare also added elements of the malcontent, a figure becoming increasingly familiar on the Elizabethan and Jacobean stage. Generally speaking, the malcontent was a character of abilities superior to those he encountered, but of inferior social status. As a result of this situation he became bitterly envious, and tended to generate a satirical commentary on the world in which he functioned. The malcontent's envy was usually given some semblance of moral justification however, while Thersites' envy is universal and indiscriminate; he mocks folly and stupidity, but he also mocks what is good, and is absolutely without sympathy for human suffering or belief in human benevolence.

Thersites is the representative of the satiric vision, and his major function is to provide a vituperative commentary on the actions of the Greek leaders. His language, aggressive though it is, is full of energy and is often very amusing, but his attacks are motivated by envy, as he recognizes himself, and many critics think that because of this the authority of what he says is discredited. Nevertheless, his harsh comments often demonstrate real perceptions about the nature of his victims. Achilles' misplaced pride, which Ulysses tries at great length to show him, is neatly summarized by Thersites' 'thou picture of what thou seemest, and idol of idiot worshippers' (V.1.6–7). He has the talent of being able in a few words to present a new perspective on a character: to call Ulysses a 'dog-fox' (V.4.11) is to draw attention to the cunning that is certainly a part of Ulysses' intelligence. None of the Greek leaders escapes his sharp tongue, and even when his comments are cruel they can be witty; the comic long-windedness of wise old Nestor may very well bring to mind a 'stale old mouse-eaten dry cheese' (V.4.10), and having seen for ourselves the limited intelligence of the great and godlike Agamemnon we can see a point to Thersites' view that 'he has not so much brain as ear-wax' (V.1.49–50).

It is clear from this violently disrespectful treatment of the Greek leaders that Thersites is in the play to deflate their pretensions, discrediting their elevated language with a demotic rhetoric of his own that is filled with animal imagery as well as with images of bodily appetites and of sickness. Like Ulysses, he uses language in an attempt to exert power, but otherwise he is in absolute opposition to Ulysses, as committed to creating disorder as the latter is to creating order; he is, almost, the embodiment of the disease that Ulysses has identified as the cause of the Greek failure. He works to dismantle hierarchy by pulling down its head, matching the leaders, as Nestor says, 'in comparisons with dirt'

(I.3.194). His first words, inflicting a plague of boils on Agamemnon, perform precisely this function. Thersites sees clearly how hierarchy works as a political instrument of control, as he points out to Achilles and Ajax: 'There's Ulysses and old Nestor ... yoke you like draught-oxen, and make you plough up the war' (II.1.103–6). He counters this by constructing inverted hierarchies, such as his hierarchy of folly: 'Agamemnon is a fool to offer to command Achilles, Achilles is a fool to be commanded of Agamemnon, Thersites is a fool to serve such a fool, and Patroclus is a fool positive' (II.3.61–4). Even more potent is his inverted hierarchy of beasts, which places Menelaus at the bottom, lower than 'the louse of a lazar' (V.1.61).

Thersites' mockery spills over into the love-plot in V.2. His commentary on the attempt of Troilus to come to terms with the new reality of an unfaithful Cressida by trying to deny it is as perceptive as we have come to expect: 'Will he swagger himself out on's own eyes?' (V.2.139). He is at his least acceptable when he considers the tormented disillusionment of Troilus, but his cruel glee comes about because he sees all action, whether of the warrior or the lover, as arising from the basest of motives: 'Lechery, lechery, still wars and lechery; nothing else holds fashion!' (V.2.197–8). His cynical attitude may be unattractive, but it does at least rest on an assumption that the world should be better than it is, and if his vision frequently seems to distort the world of the play, it also frequently reveals a truth about it.

The fact that he reveals these truths does not mean that Thersites represents Shakespeare's point of view, any more than Ulysses does. Like Ulysses, he represents a perspective that has its limitations but that makes us question other perspectives also. His motivation, certainly, is ignoble, as he himself well knows, for he sums up his own failings as uncompromisingly as he does the failings of those he mocks: 'I am a rascal, a scurvy railing knave, a very filthy rogue' (V.4.28–9). Still, he speaks for all those who perceive themselves to be victims of power, and for those who, asserting the freedom of intelligence, refuse to be taken in by false rhetoric and false images. Within the play, only the vitriolic tongue of Thersites punishes folly and vice. He frequently lays the curse of disease on the world, of the dry serpigo or the Neapolitan bone-ache, but he knows that folly is its own punishment: as he says to Patroclus, 'thyself upon thyself! The common curse of mankind, folly and ignorance, be thine in great revenue!' (II.3.26–8). 'Thyself upon thyself', indeed, the punishment of being what you are, is the most extreme punishment that the play holds out for everyone, from Thersites himself, lost in the labyrinth of his fury, to Achilles, turned into a melodramatic monster, to Troilus, Cressida and Pandarus, ironically defining their own folly through their own future reputations.

Although the satiric vision dominates much of the play, the final words are given to the comic figure, Pandarus. With a lack of comprehension that is quite characteristic, he wonders at the nature of the world that has rewarded his efforts as pandar with nothing but ingratitude, and as he has done on other occasions he tries to give his experience a meaning through a verse of a popular song. He goes on, however, in another tone altogether when he mocks the audience for showing the symptoms of syphilis and accuses them of being pandars and whores, finally cursing them with his own (no doubt venereal) diseases:

> Till then I'll sweat, and seek about for eases,
> And at that time bequeath you my diseases.
> (V.10.56–7)

Here he is speaking with a voice and attitude that we associate rather with Thersites, so that the final impression of the play transforms the (already darkly) comic into the satiric, sending the audience away scratching its boils and its serpigo.

5. Language, Style and Rhetoric

The first thing to be noted about the style of *Troilus and Cressida* is the extraordinary variety of its effects. The verse ranges from the romantic lyricism of Troilus through the pompous language of Agamemnon and the more flexible, analytical verse of Ulysses to the lurid melodrama of the later verse of Achilles, while the prose can accommodate the fussy comedy of Pandarus, the wit bordering on crudity of Cressida, and the much more virulent speech of Thersites. This variety of styles is one of the causes of the complication of perspectives in the play, as elevated verse is put into violent juxtaposition with comic or satirical verse, best illustrated by the brilliant orchestration of voices in V.2, where 120 lines of fragmented verse bring together the vulnerable pleading and teasing of Cressida, the near-contemptuous brusqueness of Diomedes, the growing horror and attempted self-control of Troilus and the amazed commentary of Ulysses, all punctured by the satirical prose of Thersites. In spite of this variety, however, many critics have noted a certain thinness of poetic feeling, an apparent emptiness behind much of the language. This has sometimes been dismissed as a failure on the dramatist's part, but it is surely one of the play's intended effects.

When, near the end of the play, Cressida writes a letter to Troilus, he dismisses it as 'Words, words, mere words, no matter from the heart' (V.3.107), and at the same time dismisses her from his thoughts. But the question of the relationship between words and matter, between words and truth, does not go away and is, indeed, fundamental to the meaning of the play. Over and over again we find that words, used in an attempt to establish truth, simply obscure it. The most immediate example of this is the language of Troilus himself. It is the conventional idealizing language of the Petrarchan lover, persistently elevating the feelings it embodies:

> Cressid, I love thee in so strained a purity
> That the blest gods, as angry with my fancy,
> More bright in zeal than the devotion which
> Cold lips blow to their deities, take thee from me.
>
> (IV.4.23–6)

The characteristic abstraction of his emotions here (the idea of the strained purity of his love echoes his earlier claim to a 'winnowed purity'

81

that is related to his idea of himself as the embodiment of truth and simplicity, and looks forward to his final words to Cressida when he defines himself in terms of truth) reaches its self-aggrandizing climax when he sees himself in time to come as the pattern by which all other claims to truth will be measured:

> Yet, after all comparisons of truth,
> As truth's authentic author to be cited,
> 'As true as Troilus' shall crown up the verse,
> And sanctify the numbers.
>
> (III.2.178–81)

Whatever sympathy we may feel for such idealism, we cannot avoid noting also its absurdity. The problem is that language has become a medium to dilute and obscure meaning rather than clarify it. Troilus mocks the oaths of lovers who need to express their love with similes and 'big compare', and yet, as we have already noted of his attempt in the opening scene to define the effect of love on him, he can only do so by multiplying comparisons in which the actual feeling tends to be dissipated. His further problem is that a love such as the one he has constructed needs an object, and he constructs his image of Cressida to be that object, never seeing through his construct to the real Cressida.

There is a different kind of elevation of language in the martial scenes, most notably in the Greek debate. Agamemnon presents his analysis of the military situation in a contorted, highly Latinate rhetoric that on the one hand lends a suitably heroic tone to what he is saying, and on the other serves to disguise the fact that he has no answer to the problem:

> The ample proposition that hope makes
> In all designs begun on earth below
> Fails in the promised largeness: checks and disasters
> Grow in the veins of actions highest reared,
> As knots, by the conflux of meeting sap,
> Infect the sound pine, and divert his grain
> Tortive and errant from his course of growth.
>
> (I.3.3–9)

'Conflux' and 'tortive' are two of many coinages in this play, words invented by Shakespeare and largely associated with the martial rhetoric, which have the effect of being suggestive and obfuscatory at the same time. Agamemnon clearly thinks he is saying something here, as does Nestor who paraphrases Agamemnon's speech in an extended metaphor filled with classical references that, again, effectively obscures the fact that nothing is being said. The grandeur of the expression throughout this scene contrasts starkly with the baseness of the intention, serving primarily to ennoble a war for which the justification can be rendered down to Thersites' pithy formulation: 'All the argument is a whore and a cuckold' (II.3.71–2). We can only assume that the opening of Ulysses' first speech, which inflates Agamemnon through a series of comparisons, is intended ironically, since Ulysses is well aware of the potential of rhetoric for persuasion and manipulation. Whereas Agamemnon, like Troilus, is the victim of his own rhetoric, Ulysses knows how to employ it to victimize others by using language to distort truth; but even for him, as in his attempts to bring Achilles and Ajax into line, it is a weapon of uncertain effectiveness.

The question of the ability of language to reveal truth embraces the argument about value that goes on in the play. The concept of hierarchy presented by Ulysses supposes a fixed place for everything and therefore a fixed value and a fixed meaning. Once order disintegrates, so does the possibility of objective value and meaning, and the relativism proposed by Troilus becomes possible. 'What's ought but as 'tis valued?' The link between word and meaning slips and truth risks getting lost in a chaos of noise. This is why there is so much naming in the play; it implies that a word is its meaning, that an essence can be fixed by a name. Pandarus provides the best example of this, as he seems incapable of using any name only once:

> That's Helenus – I marvel where Troilus is – that's Helenus – I think he went not forth today – that's Helenus.

> (I.2.219–21)

Earlier in this same scene, when he is trying to stimulate Cressida's interest in Troilus, he says: 'Well, I say Troilus is Troilus' (I.2.66). It is as if he believes he has thus defined the essence of his young friend.

A related issue is the frequency with which characters describe each other, though as we have seen with the conflicting descriptions of Diomedes by Ulysses and Thersites, men do not always see the same thing, and no description is to be trusted. This is amusingly demonstrated when Helen's servant describes her to Pandarus as 'the mortal Venus, the heart-blood of beauty, love's visible soul' (I I I.1.32–3), and Pandarus takes it to be a description of Cressida. In this play there is always the possibility of such misunderstanding because all words are risky, all language is liable to distort, all styles are in conflict. Pandarus, speaking to this same servant, shows a surprisingly intelligent (or is it simply unconscious?) awareness of the liability of different styles to prevent communication: 'Friend, we understand not one another: I am too courtly, and thou art too cunning' (III.1.27–8).

While rhetorical inflation comes in the play's verse, prose is associated with deflation, and is employed chiefly by Pandarus and Thersites. In the opening scene, every attempt by Troilus to detach himself from the ground by idealization of his love is punctured by the prose of Pandarus, who matches the young man's elevating literary metaphors with insistent materialistic metaphors of his own, and finally breaks down Troilus' verse into fragments and phrases. The scene following this begins in verse, with Alexander's account of the behaviour of Hector after his defeat at the hands of Ajax. The near-grotesque description of Ajax himself seems to require prose, however, and the remainder of the scene between Cressida and Pandarus is carried on in prose, which is the natural medium for Cressida and offers an interesting comment on Troilus' idealizing endeavours of the preceding scene – that the woman he wants to make the subject of his romantic verse should be so insistently prosaic. Only Cressida's final soliloquy, in which by revealing her true feelings for Troilus she shows how far she is in control of the situation with Pandarus, is in verse, but the possibilities of elevation here are undercut by a suggestion of insincerity in the jingling of the rhymed couplets.

An even more destructive effect is achieved by the satirical prose of Thersites. Both the debate scenes are in verse, and each is followed immediately by the violent entrance of Thersites, which in each case deflates the pretensions of what has gone before. Much of the energy of the Greek debate is spent in endeavour to restore the authority of Agamemnon, but it is hard to believe in this god-like nature when we are forced to picture him covered in running boils. The deflation is effected not simply by the image, but by the impact of the colloquial prose upon the lofty pretensions of the leader's verse. A similar effect is achieved after the Trojan debate on the moral issues of the war and the value of Helen as a pretext, when Thersites puts his curse on 'those that war for a placket' (II.3.19–20). It is noteworthy in these two scenes with Thersites that Achilles and Patroclus, who elsewhere use verse, here use prose, but revert to verse when Thersites has left the scene. The counter-movement is insistent: for all the upward pretensions of their rhetoric, characters are constantly pulled downwards towards the comic or satiric.

This lends particular interest to the single scene in which we actually meet Helen (III.1), for as a result of Pandarus' presence here the scene is carried on in prose, and the trifling and superficial wit that is characteristic of the old man infects the whole scene. The few lines of verse left to

Helen and Paris after Pandarus leaves do nothing to repair the damage. Even more revealing is the effect of his presence on the meeting of the lovers in the scene which follows. All Troilus' verse has been moving towards this moment, and at the beginning of the scene he expresses his anticipation as well as his fears in a language that is similar to what we have heard from him before. The crass bluntness of Pandarus' prose, however, with its insistence on the carnality of what is happening, so affects the lovers that when he leaves them alone the moment that might have generated supreme poetic emotion produces instead an awkward and self-conscious prose.

The downward pull comes not only in the prose, but also in the play's imagery. The images fall into groups, the largest being concerned with food and cooking, but there are also many images of sickness and disease, and of the body, as well as animal imagery. The various groups are all interconnected, and tend to suggest decay, disintegration, and a transition from the human to the bestial. The first image of food is provided by Pandarus, when he treats the affair he is promoting between Troilus and Cressida as if he were baking a cake. This is, of course, comic, but it has a greater significance than this, for it lays emphasis upon the relationship between love and appetite. Troilus unconsciously makes the same association when, immediately before his meeting with Cressida, he expresses the force of his anticipation in terms of tasting:

> Th' imaginary relish is so sweet
> That it enchants my sense. What will it be,
> When that the watery palate tastes indeed
> Love's thrice-repurèd nectar?
>
> (III.2.17–20)

It is not surprising that his horror at her betrayal of him should be expressed in a culinary image of sickened appetite as he sees his love turn into garbage,

> The fragments, scraps, the bits, and greasy relics
> Of her o'er-eaten faith, are bound to Diomed.
>
> (V.2.162–3)

We can, of course, understand Troilus' revulsion, but we should consider what is implied about Troilus himself by his use of images that make Cressida an object of his appetite, for they provide a telling contrast with his attempts to spiritualize his love. It is worth noting here that during the debate about the value of Helen, when Troilus is trying to raise her also as an ideal, one of the images he uses in his arguments for retaining her associates her too with leftover food:

> ... the remainder viands
> We do not throw in unrespective sieve
> Because we now are full.
>
> (II.2.71–3)

He clearly does not recognize the inappropriateness for the point he is trying to make of the comparison here invoked, and it is a sign of his moral confusion that when he is trying to speak of what is to be valued, an image of sated appetite should spring to mind. It imparts extra meaning to Thersites' idea of rival lovers with an appetite for the same morsel devouring each other: 'What's become of the wenching rogues? I think they have swallowed one another. I would laugh at that miracle – yet, in a sort, lechery eats itself' (V.4.32–5).

Images of appetite, food and devouring connect the two plots, for they are also associated with disorder and death. Troilus considers Helen 'too starved a subject' for his sword, while after the day's battle Hector lays down his sword, which has had its 'fill of blood and death'. Achilles' sword does not have its fill until Hector is dead:

> My half-supped sword, that frankly would have fed,
> Pleased with this dainty bait, thus goes to bed.
>
> (V.8.19–20)

The occurrence of such imagery in both plots is a reminder that the war itself was provoked by appetite, by Paris' desire for the honey-sweet Helen. One man's meat is another man's poison, however, and Diomedes sees Helen only as 'contaminated carrion'. The effect of this sequence of images is to see men as favouring their baser selves, setting desire over reason, and consequently moving closer to the bestial. The total liberation of appetite is the final nightmare envisioned by Ulysses, the inevitable end of disorder leading to annihilation:

> ... appetite, an universal wolf,
> So doubly seconded with will and power,
> Must make perforce an universal prey,
> And last eat up himself.
>
> (I.3.121–4)

This vision of a world that Ulysses fears may come about is akin to the vision of the world that Thersites believes has come about, for in his satiric commentary, which generates most of the animal imagery in the play, men are constantly sliding into a bestial state: Ulysses to dog-fox, Ajax to elephant, Achilles to cur, Menelaus to bull, ass, ox, and on down the scale to a herring without a roe.

86

The imagery of disease has a similar critical function. Love that should have an integrative effect has turned Troilus' heart into an open ulcer, and descriptions of Cressida's beauty, far from providing healing medicine, are like a knife probing the wounds that love has given. This conjoining of sickness and love is taken up again in the satirical commentary of Thersites, for whom venereal disease, the literal open ulcer caused by love, is a major weapon in the armoury of diseases he would lay like a curse upon those that 'war for a placket'. Paradoxically, for him disease is a kind of medicine, since it is used against moral sickness: the Neapolitan bone-ache is a cure for lechery, and he would cure the folly and ignorance of mankind with boils, red murrain, dry serpigo, and a surgeon's box full of other bitter pills: 'the rotten diseases of the south, guts-griping ruptures, catarrhs, loads o' gravel i' th' back, lethargies, cold palsies, and the like' (V.1.17–20). Images of sickness in the physical body mimic moral sickness and the sickness in the social body, the disorder that Ulysses has diagnosed and wants to cure. Order is health,

> And therefore is the glorious planet Sol
> In noble eminence enthroned and sphered
> Amidst the other, whose med'cinable eye
> Corrects the ill aspects of planets evil . . .
> (I.3.89–92)

It is only one more of the ironies of this play that the figure to whom Ulysses' concern with the diagnosis of sickness most closely relates him should be Thersites.

If we return to the question of the emptiness that critics have felt lies behind some of the language of the play, we can now see that it has a number of causes. It can be the result of the efforts of characters to dignify the undignified, to clothe mundane ideas in high-sounding language, or to elevate themselves by grand rhetorical gestures, as with the Greek leaders. Or it can be the result of a faulty vision of the world and the creation of illusions, as with Troilus. It may be used to conceal its purposes, like the apparently effective rhetoric of Ulysses, and even then may not achieve its end. For many of the characters, rhetoric itself may seem to be a disease. Troilus hardly knows when to stop speaking, and his most effective moment may well be the single line he speaks when he finally meets Cressida: 'You have bereft me of all words, lady' (III.2.53). His penultimate speech is much more characteristic: he gives a moving account of the effects of the death of Hector, which he concludes with the simple words: 'Hector is dead;

there is no more to say' (V.10.22). This would have been a fine line with which to end the play but, being Troilus, he finds more to say: nine lines of bombast in which he recreates himself as revenger, as he had once created himself as lover.

6. Time and Theatre

Time

> Time doth transfix the flourish set on youth,
> And delves the parallels in beauty's brow,
> Feeds on the rarities of nature's truth,
> And nothing stands but for his scythe to mow.

The theme of mutability, the melancholy fact that all things will fall to the ravages of time, finds frequent memorable expression in Shakespeare's works, as in these lines from Sonnet 60. Time is the enemy of all man's attempts to find something of permanent value, and it is hardly surprising that the idea of time should appear in none of his plays with as much insistence as in *Troilus and Cressida*. The fall of Troy, a topic of major interest to the Elizabethans because of the supposed connection of the ancient civilization to their own history, was a demonstration of the inexorable workings of time to make an end to even the greatest of civilizations, and to render futile the delusory attempts that men make to defeat time by living on in reputation.

The play's major philosophical statement about time is given to Ulysses. Although in this speech Ulysses uses ideas about mutability not for their intrinsic truth, but for the quite specific purpose of moving Achilles from his sloth, his account of time as devourer, as destroyer of everything that men value, makes a significant comment on all that happens in the play:

> Time hath, my lord, a wallet at his back,
> Wherein he puts alms for oblivion,
> A great-sized monster of ingratitudes:
> Those scraps are good deeds past, which are devoured
> As fast as they are made, forgot as soon
> As done . . .
> For beauty, wit,
> High birth, vigour of bone, desert in service,
> Love, friendship, charity, are subjects all
> To envious and calumniating time.
>
> (III.3.145–50, 171–4)

What Ulysses says here about time is, in a sense, actually a comment on

89

the inconstant attitudes of men. Although in the long term time will consign to oblivion everything that exists, in the short term it is the ingratitude of men that consigns good deeds to oblivion as they forget about what they once valued in favour of a newer fashion. This is why time is personified as a figure who embodies many of the negative impulses of the play. The idea of time as a devourer links the figure to the imagery of food and to the destructive human appetites that drive so many of the characters. There is an irony in the fact that Ulysses uses the phrase 'great-sized monster' in this context, for there is an echo of the phrase at the end of the play when Achilles, to whom he uses it, is called a 'great-sized coward' by Troilus. Envy, in the form of emulation, is a recurrent theme, and the idea of time as an envious calumniator inevitably brings Thersites to mind. Time, that is, is not seen in abstract terms, but as a figure containing elements of human aggression and instability.

Because of his own immediate loss, Troilus' concern with devouring time is personal rather than philosophical:

> Injurious Time now, with a robber's haste,
> Crams his rich thievery up, he knows not how;
> As many farewells as be stars in heaven,
> With distinct breath and consigned kisses to them,
> He fumbles up into a loose adieu,
> And scants us with a single famished kiss,
> Distasted with the salt of broken tears.
>
> (IV.4.41–7)

The idea of time as the destroyer of all that is beautiful or valuable is matter for tragedy, but the association of the figure of time by both Ulysses and Troilus with human vices and weaknesses adds a satirical dimension to the image, for change is not simply a matter of time, but also of human frailty and instability of purpose. If it is the case, as Ulysses says, that time will destroy Achilles' reputation, it is also the case that Achilles' own sloth will contribute to that destruction. Time and his own nature will make the hero Achilles into a murderer. Time, in effect, reveals the inconstancy of human nature, the weakness of human motives, the futility of human endeavour, and uncovers a truth that is in opposition to the idea of 'truth' that Troilus would embrace. Cressida believes that she can be 'true' in the way that Troilus expects:

> Make Cressid's name the very crown of falsehood
> If ever she leave Troilus! Time, force, and death,
> Do to this body what extremity you can . . .
>
> (IV.2.99–101)

Time, in the form of reputation, will indeed make her name the crown of falsehood, rendering truth the reverse of what she intends. Time turns her into a whore, but only by revealing the reality of her own pliable vulnerability; it simply allows the working-out of her character. Many of the characters of *Troilus and Cressida* are concerned with protecting reputation (or honour, as the Trojans think of it) as a means of defeating the limitations that time imposes on men. Shakespeare, looking back at them through time, could see how far they had succeeded in this; so, at the end of III.2, he made Cressida, Troilus and Pandarus step forward and look through history at the reputations that they ironically hoped time would give them. The Greek and Trojan heroes had a more justified faith in reputation, since time turned them for Shakespeare's age into symbols of courtesy, heroism, wisdom, intelligence. Yet in a way, by writing this play about them Shakespeare played a terrible joke on them. By deflating the reputations of the ancient heroes, he was himself changing their meaning in time – contributing, in effect, to their mutability.

Theatre

The theatre itself, or perhaps rather the theatricality of life, is the subject of many of Shakespeare's plays, but there is probably none in which the metaphor of theatre is so pervasive as *Troilus and Cressida*, where the characters are constantly acting out roles, or directing the performances of others, or being made into spectators. The play suggests that identity may be nothing more than a role. In the opening scene we see Troilus, by means of Petrarchan rhetoric, unconsciously creating himself as the conventional literary lover, a role into which he fits himself for most of the play. Ulysses is much more consciously an actor, well aware that his rhetorical performances, however plausible, are essentially fictions constructed with the purpose of affecting a particular audience. Cressida is sometimes conscious that she is playing a part, as when she plays the indifferent, hard-to-seem-won woman for Pandarus and Troilus; at other times she appears to be unaware that she is acting, as when she presents herself as the embodiment of eternal constancy. Ajax is first presented to us, in Alexander's description (I.2.19–30), as being made up of incongruous bits and pieces, and only finds an identity for himself when he is playing the part of Achilles. These are characters who are playing themselves or, perhaps, trying to find selves to play. Others, like Thersites and Patroclus, can distance themselves from the parts they play by using the theatricality of theatre.

If *Troilus and Cressida* is about actors, it is also about audiences, about people watching other people, turning them into spectacle. Helen and Hecuba climb to the tower to watch the battle, Pandarus and Cressida observe the pageant of the returning warriors. Pandarus becomes a voyeur to the love-play of Troilus and Cressida, and later is witness to their grief: 'What a pair of spectacles is here!' (IV.4.13) he says, with as much relish of the scene as pity for their suffering. Greeks and Trojans watch the combat of Hector and Ajax, which indeed turns out to be nothing more than a performance. And Troilus watches Cressida and Diomedes in a kind of morality play, a piece of didactic theatre from which he learns less than he might have learned. In these cases it is the spectators who create the theatre, since the actors are not aware that they *are* theatre. In the scene of the meeting between Troilus and Cressida, Pandarus turns their love into theatre in a different way: by treating Cressida's actions as if they were a performance and instructing the lovers on how to act, he succeeds in making the whole meeting awkward and artificial.

Ulysses is the most active creator of theatre. He sees the importance of illusion for establishing and maintaining authority, and tries to use theatre as an instrument for a manipulation that is essentially political. He creates two performances that are intended to redirect the pride of Achilles so that he will return to his position in the hierarchy. In the first (II.3), the Greek leaders perform for Ajax and convince him of his superiority over Achilles in an attempt to provoke Achilles to rejoin the combat and reassert his pre-eminence. In the second (III.3), with the same purpose in mind, they pretend to ignore Achilles so that Ulysses can show him that his reputation is in decline. Neither performance has the effect that Ulysses intends. While Ulysses tries to employ theatre as an instrument of authority, Patroclus and Thersites use it rather more effectively for the opposite political purpose. For them, theatre is essentially satirical and subversive. The account that Ulysses gives during the Greek debate of Patroclus' mimicry of Agamemnon and Nestor (an account that is itself a calculated piece of theatre intended to enrage the leaders) makes it clear that such theatre is dangerous, since it encourages disrespect and undermines order. Thersites creates a similar destructive form of theatre: the impersonation of Ajax that he gives for Achilles (III.3) has more effect on Achilles than does the drama arranged by Ulysses that immediately precedes it.

It is Ulysses' recognition of the potentially dangerous effectiveness of theatre that provokes his attack on the acting of Patroclus, an attack that may seem paradoxical considering the extensiveness of his own theatrical projects:

> And with ridiculous and awkward action –
> Which, slanderer, he imitation calls –
> He pageants us. Sometimes, great Agamemnon,
> Thy topless deputation he puts on,
> And like a strutting player whose conceit
> Lies in his hamstring, and doth think it rich
> To hear the wooden dialogue and sound
> 'Twixt his stretched footing and the scaffoldage,
> Such to-be-pitied and o'er-wrested seeming
> He acts thy greatness in . . .

> (I.3.149–58)

What lies behind Ulysses' attack is a fear of theatre that is used in what he considers to be an irresponsible manner, but this attitude is especially ironic if we consider the irresponsibility of his own cruellest piece of theatre, in which he organizes the humiliation of Cressida by having her kissed in general, thus creating the conditions that allow him to define her as a daughter of the game. He appears there to have reached a point where, for him, theatre and reality have merged.

Coda: Time and Theatre

Time, we might say, is the stage upon which the actors of *Troilus and Cressida* have to play their parts. The image of the world as a stage on which man is merely an actor is a common one in Shakespearean drama, both comic and tragic. The best-known statement of the idea in a comedy is probably that of Jaques in *As You Like It* (1600?), in which he defines the seven ages of man as a series of dramatic roles:

> All the world's a stage,
> And all the men and women merely players;
> They have their exits and their entrances,
> And one man in his time plays many parts . . .

Jaques is essentially a satirist, and his description is mocking and reductive. The most familiar use of the image in a tragedy comes in *Macbeth* (1605–6?):

> Life's but a walking shadow, a poor player
> That struts and frets his hour upon the stage
> And then is heard no more.

Macbeth's version of the idea is more painful than that of Jaques because it acknowledges more keenly the element of futility given to man's life by the tyranny of time. What makes the image of man as actor so potent and potentially tragic is just this sense of an ephemeral and doomed activity.

The pervasive theatricality of the manner in which *Troilus and Cressida* dramatizes the events that hastened the end of a great civilization, and the preoccupation of the participants in those events with time, and especially with a future in which they will long have ceased to exist, account in part for the play's overwhelming sense of transience. Theatre itself, as Jaques and Macbeth both recognize, offers only illusion, a timeless moment that is immediately lost in time. When the dramatist took an event out of ancient history and re-created it for an Elizabethan audience, he made history itself into an illusion. Like the play's concern with the problematical connection between word and matter, between name and identity, its theatrical imagery implies that reality, of which history is a part, is a construct. And if reality is perceived as being only illusion, that perception itself must lead to disillusionment, which is the tone that most readers identify in the play. The play's theatricality has the effect of draining away the characters' identity, making them seem to be nothing more than the roles they are playing at the particular moment, and this deprives the play of tragic emotion and contributes a further bitterness to the disillusionment. This bitterness associated with the play's treatment of posturing and superficiality has led some critics to see the play as evidence of Shakespeare's own disillusionment with the theatre, though we must remember that the anti-theatrical attitude is ambiguously associated with Ulysses, who has good reason to fear the power of theatre at the same time as he uses that power. Perhaps the disillusionment is with history and politics rather than with theatre.

One of the undeniable effects of the play's theatricality is to offer an image of the smallness of Greeks and Trojans as they play their little parts on the great stage of time, and so to diminish the stature of the heroic mythical figures and reveal the pettiness of their political motivation. One can, of course, claim that this is a universal image of the predicament of all men, and in a sense it is. But the play's primary meaning was for its own time, and it must have held out a mocking example to the heroes and politicians of the competing patriarchies of New Troy, 'strutting players' around a queen who, like Helen, had been 'a theme of honour and renown,/A spur to valiant and magnanimous deeds' (II.2.200–201), whose own court was a great stage, whose obsession with illusion and theatricality was immense, and whose performance on the great stage of England was so shortly to come to an end.

Select Bibliography

NOTE: All quotations are from the New Penguin edition of *Troilus and Cressida*, ed. R. A. Foakes, Harmondsworth, 1987.

Editions

Troilus and Cressida, ed. Kenneth Muir. The Oxford Shakespeare, Oxford, 1982.
Troilus and Cressida, ed. Kenneth Palmer. The Arden Shakespeare, London and New York, 1982.

Sources

GEOFFREY BULLOUGH *Narrative and Dramatic Sources of Shakespeare*, Volume VI, London, 1966.
KENNETH MUIR *The Sources of Shakespeare's Plays*, London, 1977.

Background

OSCAR J. CAMPBELL *'Comicall Satyre' and Shakespeare's 'Troilus and Cressida'*, San Marino, Calif., 1938.
JULIET DUSINBERRE *Shakespeare and the Nature of Women*, London, 1975.
GRAHAM HOLDERNESS *Shakespeare's History*, Dublin and New York, 1985.
JILL LEVENSON 'Shakespeare's *Troilus and Cressida* and the Monumental Tradition in Tapestries and Literature', *Renaissance Drama* 7, 1976, pp. 43–83.
ROBERT K. PRESSON *Shakespeare's 'Troilus and Cressida' and the Legends of Troy*, Madison, Wis., 1953.
ISABEL RIVERS *Classical and Christian Ideas in English Renaissance Poetry*, London, 1979. (See esp. pp. 57–92.)
ANN THOMPSON *Shakespeare's Chaucer: A Study in Literary Origins*, London, 1978.
E. M. W. TILLYARD *The Elizabethan World Picture*, London, 1943.

On Shakespeare and *Troilus and Cressida*

S. L. BETHELL *Shakespeare and the Popular Dramatic Tradition*, London, 1944.
M. M. BURNS '*Troilus and Cressida*: The Worst of Both Worlds', *Shakespeare Studies* 13, 1980, pp. 105–30.
T. EAGLETON *Shakespeare and Society*, London, 1967.
PHILIP EDWARDS *Shakespeare and the Confines of Art*, London, 1968.

Critical Studies: Troilus and Cressida

R. A. FOAKES *Shakespeare, the Dark Comedies to the Last Plays. From Satire to Celebration,* London, 1971.

NORTHROP FRYE *Fools of Time,* London, 1968.

SIDNEY HOMAN *Shakespeare's Theatre of Presence,* Lewisburg, 1986.

ROBERT KIMBROUGH *Shakespeare's 'Troilus and Cressida' and Its Setting,* Cambridge, Mass., 1964.

G. WILSON KNIGHT *The Wheel of Fire,* London, 1930.

W. W. LAWRENCE *Shakespeare's Problem Comedies,* New York, 1931.

DERICK R. C. MARSH 'Interpretation and Misinterpretation: the Problem of *Troilus and Cressida',* Shakespeare Studies 1, 1965, pp. 182–98.

PRISCILLA MARTIN (ed.) *Shakespeare: 'Troilus and Cressida': A Casebook,* London, 1976. (Brings together a number of useful essays and extracts.)

NORMAN RABKIN *Shakespeare and the Common Understanding,* New York, 1967.

A. P. ROSSITER *Angel with Horns,* London, 1961.

E. M. W. TILLYARD *Shakespeare's Problem Plays,* London, 1950.

FOR THE BEST IN PAPERBACKS, LOOK FOR THE

In every corner of the world, on every subject under the sun, Penguin represents quality and variety – the very best in publishing today.

For complete information about books available from Penguin – including Pelicans, Puffins, Peregrines and Penguin Classics – and how to order them, write to us at the appropriate address below. Please note that for copyright reasons the selection of books varies from country to country.

In the United Kingdom: Please write to *Dept E.P., Penguin Books Ltd, Harmondsworth, Middlesex, UB7 0DA*

If you have any difficulty in obtaining a title, please send your order with the correct money, plus ten per cent for postage and packaging, to *PO Box No 11, West Drayton, Middlesex*

In the United States: Please write to *Dept BA, Penguin, 299 Murray Hill Parkway, East Rutherford, New Jersey 07073*

In Canada: Please write to *Penguin Books Canada Ltd, 2801 John Street, Markham, Ontario L3R 1B4*

In Australia: Please write to the *Marketing Department, Penguin Books Australia Ltd, P.O. Box 257, Ringwood, Victoria 3134*

In New Zealand: Please write to the *Marketing Department, Penguin Books (NZ) Ltd, Private Bag, Takapuna, Auckland 9*

In India: Please write to *Penguin Overseas Ltd, 706 Eros Apartments, 56 Nehru Place, New Delhi, 110019*

In Holland: Please write to *Penguin Books Nederland B.V., Postbus 195, NL–1380AD Weesp, Netherlands*

In Germany: Please write to *Penguin Books Ltd, Friedrichstrasse 10–12, D–6000 Frankfurt Main 1, Federal Republic of Germany*

In Spain: Please write to *Longman Penguin España, Calle San Nicolas 15, E–28013 Madrid, Spain*

In France: Please write to *Penguin Books Ltd, 39 Rue de Montmorency, F-75003, Paris, France*

In Japan: Please write to *Longman Penguin Japan Co Ltd, Yamaguchi Building, 2–12–9 Kanda Jimbocho, Chiyoda-Ku, Tokyo 101, Japan*

FOR THE BEST IN PAPERBACKS, LOOK FOR THE 🐧

PENGUIN SELF-STARTERS

Self-Starters is a new series designed to help you develop skills and proficiency in the subject of your choice. Each book has been written by an expert and is suitable for school-leavers, students, those considering changing their career in mid-stream and all those who study at home.

Titles published or in preparation:

Accounting	Noel Trimming
Advertising	Michael Pollard
Basic Statistics	Peter Gwilliam
A Career in Banking	Sheila Black, John Brennan
Clear English	Vivian Summers
French	Anne Stevens
German	Anna Nyburg
Good Business Communication	Doris Wheatley
Marketing	Marsaili Cameron, Angela Rushton, David Carson
Nursing	David White
Personnel Management	J. D. Preston
Public Relations	Sheila Black, John Brennan
Public Speaking	Vivian Summers
Retailing	David Couch
Secretarial Skills	Gale Cornish, Charlotte Coudrille, Joan Lipkin-Edwardes
Starting a Business on a Shoestring	Michel Syrett, Chris Dunn
Understanding Data	Peter Sprent

FOR THE BEST IN PAPERBACKS, LOOK FOR THE 🐧

PENGUIN PASSNOTES

This comprehensive series, deisgned to help GCSE students, includes:

SUBJECTS
Biology
Chemistry
Economics
English Language
Geography
Human Biology
Mathematics
Modern Mathematics
Modern World History
Narrative Poems
Nursing

SHAKESPEARE
As You Like It
Henry IV Part I
Henry V
Julius Caesar
Macbeth
The Merchant of Venice
A Midsummer Night's Dream
Romeo and Juliet
Twelfth Night

LITERATURE
Across the Barricades
Arms and the Man
Billy Liar
Cider with Rosie
Great Expectations
Gregory's Girl
I am the Cheese
Jane Eyre
Joby
Journey's End
Kes
Lord of the Flies
A Man for All Seasons
The Mayor of Casterbridge
My Family and Other Animals
Pride and Prejudice
The Prologue to the Canterbury
    Tales
Pygmalion
Roots
Saint Joan
She Stoops to Conquer
Silas Marner
To Kill a Mockingbird
War of the Worlds
The Woman in White
Wuthering Heights
Z for Zachariah

PLAYS IN PENGUIN

Edward Albee **Who's Afraid of Virginia Woolf?**

Alan Ayckbourn **The Norman Conquests**

Bertolt Brecht **Parables for the Theatre (The Good Woman of Setzuan/The Caucasian Chalk Circle)**

Anton Checkhov **Plays (The Cherry Orchard/The Three Sisters/Ivanov/The Seagull/Uncle Vanya)**

Vladimir Gubaryev **Sarcophagus**

Henrik Ibsen **Hedda Gabler/Pillar of Society/The Wild Duck**

Eugène Ionesco **Absurd Drama (Rhinoceros/The Chair/The Lesson)**

Ben Jonson **Three Comedies (Volpone/The Alchemist/Bartholomew Fair)**

D. H. Lawrence **Three Plays (The Collier's Friday Night/The Daughter-in-Law/The Widowing of Mrs Holroyd)**

Federico García Lorca **Three Tragedies**

Arthur Miller **Death of a Salesman**

John Mortimer **A Voyage Round My Father/What Shall We Tell Caroline?/The Dock Brief**

J. B. Priestly **Time and the Conways/I Have Been Here Before/An Inspector Calls/The Linden Tree**

Peter Shaffer **Amadeus/Equus**

Bernard Shaw **Plays Pleasant (Arms and the Man/Candida/The Man of Destiny/You Never Can Tell)**

Sophocles **Three Theban Plays (Oedipus the King/Antigone/Oedipus at Colonus)**

Arnold Wesker **The Wesker Trilogy (Chicken Soup with Barley/Roots/I'm Talking about Jerusalem)**

Oscar Wilde **Plays (Lady Windermere's Fan/A Woman of No Importance/An Ideal Husband/The Importance of Being Earnest/Salome)**

Thornton Wilder **Our Town/The Skin of Our Teeth/The Matchmaker**

Tennessee Williams **Sweet Bird of Youth/A Streetcar Named Desire/The Glass Menagerie**

FOR THE BEST IN PAPERBACKS, LOOK FOR THE 🐧

PENGUIN CRITICAL STUDIES

Described by *The Times Educational Supplement* as 'admirable' and 'superb', Penguin Critical Studies is a specially developed series of critical essays on the major works of literature for use by students in universities, colleges and schools.

Titles published or in preparation:

Antony and Cleopatra	Kenneth Muir
As You Like It	Peter Reynolds
The Great Gatsby	Kathleen Parkinson
Jane Eyre	Susie Campbell
Mansfield Park	Isobel Armstrong
Return of the Native	J. Garver
Rosenkrantz and Guildenstern are Dead	Roger Sales
Shakespeare's History Plays	C. W. R. D. Moseley
The Tempest	Sandra Clark
Tennyson	Roger Ebbatson
A Winter's Tale	Christopher Hardman
The Miller's Tale	John Cunningham
The Waste Land	Stephen Coote
The Nun's Priest's Tale	Stephen Coote
King Lear	Kenneth Muir
Othello	Gāmini and Fenella Salgādo